KENWORTH

The First 75 Years

Doug Siefkes

Documentary Book Publishers

Seattle, Washington

**Title page:
Kenworth model
T2000.**

Kenworth
The First 75 Years

Copyright 1998 by Doug Siefkes and Kenworth Truck Company
All rights reserved. No portion of this book may be reproduced or utilized in any form,
or by any electronic, mechanical or other means, without the prior written permission
of the publisher.

Photo Credits:
Kenworth: The First 75 Years would not have been possible without the generous contri-
butions of the photographers whose images appear throughout the book. Special
acknowledgment and thanks go to Walter Hodges, Doug Landreth, Ben Marra, Craig
Sherbourne, and especially Studio 3, Inc., photographers Jim Felt, Henry Ngan, and
Craig Wagner, whose work has defined Kenworth's image over the last 25 years.

Printed in Canada
Distributed in the United States by Sasquatch Books
Distributed in Canada by Raincoast Books Ltd.

Author: Doug Siefkes
Editor: Don Graydon
Copy editor: Sherri Schultz
Cover and interior design: Gary LaComa
Publisher: Barry Provorse

Library of Congress Cataloging-in-Publication Data
    LC# 97-45240

Siefkes, Doug 1959-
Kenworth: The First 75 Years

ISBN 0-935503-21-8

1. Kenworth trucks—History. 2. Kenworth Truck Company—History. I. Title.

Documentary Book Publishers
A Division of Sasquatch Books
615 Second Avenue
Seattle, Washington 98104   e-mail: docbooks@SasquatchBooks.com
(206) 467-4300   http://www.SasquatchBooks.com

Documentary Book Publishers publishes books for corporate and institutional clients
across North America. For more information about our titles and services, contact us
at the address listed above, or view our site on the World Wide Web.

CONTENTS

FOREWORD

Since the development of trade and commerce, merchants have needed to move their products from the factory to their customers. For centuries, land-based shipments traveled predominantly by horse-drawn wagon. Later, the iron horse of the railroads was preeminent. Now, less than 100 years after their creation, trucks dominate the transportation industry.

Seventy-five years ago, the trucking industry was still in its infancy. Early truck builders were pioneers who helped shape the economic landscape of the twentieth century. Leading the industry in the West with product innovation and strength was the Kenworth Truck Company.

Throughout its history, Kenworth has been defined by two hallmarks: quality and innovation. Quality drives every Kenworth operation, from design and production to customer support and services. Its manufacturing facilities have all achieved the highest international recognition for quality, ISO 9001 certification.

Innovation — whether it was producing the first factory-installed diesel engine-powered truck in 1933; building the first truly aerodynamic truck, the T600A, in 1985; or moving into the next millennium with the industry's state-of-the-art truck, the T2000 — has always been a challenge worth taking for Kenworth.

PACCAR takes pride in Kenworth's legacy of achievement and excellence. One of the highlights of PACCAR's own history is the acquisition of Kenworth in 1945.

Kenworth's powerful history will drive its future, one filled with challenge, opportunity, and achievement. Congratulations to Kenworth Truck Company on its Diamond Anniversary, and to its employees, dealers, owners, drivers, and suppliers, thank you for your contributions to its success.

Mark Pigott

Mark Pigott
Chairman and CEO
PACCAR Inc.

7

CHAPTER ONE

INVENTING A TRUCK

Bargain hunters at a wrecking yard in Federal Way, Washington, in 1984 may have ignored the rusted old truck as a useless relic, a 2-ton workhorse on its last legs. But Buster Arnestad saw it through different eyes. What a marvel of technology this forerunner of the Kenworth truck must have been when it first went to work in 1917.

Attention to detail shone in the truck's wood-spoked wheels and solid rubber tires, in its brass muffler and gearshift. Top speed had been 15 miles per hour—not bad for 1917. The nameplate was stamped "Gersix"—one of the first truck makers to give horses and wagons, and sometimes even trains, a run for their money.

Buster, a longshoreman with a lifelong fascination with old cars and trucks, couldn't believe his luck. The truck's owner, Bob Brown, headed the Northwest chapter of the American Truck Historical Society, but he had given up hopes of restoring the vehicle himself. Buster jumped at the chance to bring the sixty-seven-year-old Gersix back to life. He wrote out a check to Brown, exchanged handshakes with him, and hauled the truck away.

Buster went on to restore the old truck and later sold it to Del Hewitt, another man who appreciates historic vehicles. And when Hewitt loaned the restored Gersix No. 42 for public display at the Pacific Northwest Truck Museum in Wilsonville, Oregon, the United States gained a strong link to the earliest history of its trucking industry.

9

10

THE GERSIX TRUCK was born in Portland, Oregon, the creation of a repair shop looking for a way to fill the spare time of its employees. Mechanic J. E. Hahn recalled that truck building was one way to keep the shop at Gerlinger Motor Car Company busy when business was slow, and in 1914, business was slow most of the time.

Edward Gerlinger gave shop foreman George Peters the job of designing the company's first truck. The design was a practical one, based on available parts. Unable to use pressed-steel frames due to the high cost of dies and stamping, Peters and Hahn employed structural steel as a foundation for the truck. It proved to be a happy circumstance because the structural steel chassis was stronger and more durable than one made of pressed steel.

The next stroke of genius, or perhaps luck, was the choice of engine. Most American trucks featured four-cylinder engines, but they were hard to come by. So Peters chose a six-cylinder Continental engine. It turned out to be just the thing for the tough demands on a truck in the western United States. The new vehicle was named the Gersix, after the Gerlinger Motor Car Company and the truck's six-cylinder engine.

Page 8: A 1925 split windshield model Kenworth.

Previous page: A newly completed Gersix in front of Gerlinger Motor Car Company's Tacoma, Washington, truck manufacturing plant.

Even with no cab or bed, the first truck took more than a year to complete between repair jobs in the Gerlinger shop. It was sold as a chassis to a local brick hauler, who promptly drove it all around Portland to show it off. While that Gersix surely drew the attention of the local townsfolk, it also caught the eye of a Tacoma, Washington, investor on the lookout for a good manufacturing tenant. Gerlinger negotiated a stock-for-rent swap and in 1916 began manufacturing trucks in a small building on Fife Street in Tacoma.

Gersix trucks, with their strong frame, suspension, and drive train and their six-cylinder engine, quickly demonstrated their advantages over trucks from East Coast manufacturers. This stout "Western truck" was clearly designed for rutted roads, steep hills, heavy loads, and long hauls.

There weren't many motorized vehicles in the Pacific Northwest back then. Though gas-powered vehicles were growing in popularity, the rain-soaked Northwest was still horse country. Even the tough Gersix had its problems on country roads not well suited to heavy rigs with hard-rubber tires. "The trucks didn't have a windshield or cab, so you were just exposed to the rain," Ed Hahn recalled. "If you got off on a muddy side road, those solid tires would get to spinning and then you were in a mess."

The Gerlinger company expanded its line to sell and service Pathfinder, Holly, Menominee, and Federal trucks, as well as Vim delivery vans, and it operated an agency in Seattle. When the market seemed not quite ready to embrace trucks in a big way, Gerlinger mechanics shifted their attention to

Gersix Motor Company's showroom in Tacoma, Washington, 1916.

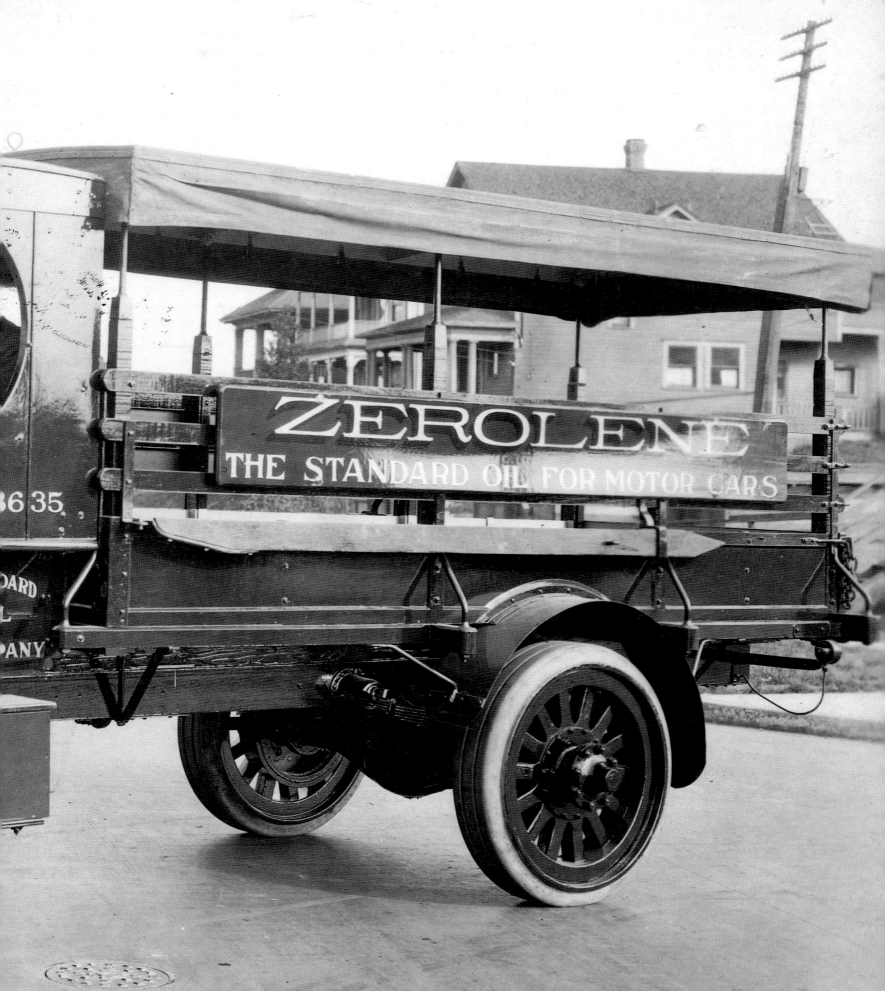

tractors. They began working on a kit to convert automobiles to tractors—the Gerlinger Tractor, as it was later advertised. Despite all this effort, the company's cash eventually dried up, and it declared bankruptcy in 1917.

The Gersix was down but not out. Gerlinger's Seattle landlord, timber baron Edgar Worthington, went in with businessman Frederick Keen, a former Coast Guard captain, to reincorporate the bankrupt operation. Both men had prospered from their interest in Washington Tug and Barge. With a few partially completed trucks and a small inventory of parts, Gersix resumed production. And on December 31, 1917, Gersix No. 42—the truck purchased many years later by Buster Arnestad—was delivered to the Overland Truck Company of Seattle.

TRUCKS CARRYING the Gersix nameplate cost a lot of money for that time: nearly $2,000. Keen and Worthington often financed part of the cost, and they accepted trade-ins, usually teams of horses and wagons. The Pacific Northwest now was home to a number of small truck builders like Gersix. A typical shop was likely to have several trucks in various stages of construction, sitting on blocks as they waited for wheels, engines, rear ends, or other components. The Federal Highway Act of 1916 meant highway development in the West would be accelerated, and prospects for the builders looked bright.

With the entry of the United States into World War I in 1917, however, dreams of new highways in the West were put on hold. Military procurement stepped up rapidly, and parts for anything—especially trucks—became increasingly scarce.

The Gersix 2½-ton model shown came with a one-year warranty, provided that the truck had not, among other things, been driven "beyond its factory rated speed." New, the chassis sold for $2,850 F.O.B. Seattle.

The Continental six-cylinder engines were no longer available, so Gersix trucks began using four-cylinder Buda and, when available, six-cylinder Wisconsin engines. When the supply of axles dried up, Gersix built its own. The 36-inch tires needed for the trucks (4 inches wide on the front wheels, 6 or 8 inches wide in the rear) were nearly impossible to buy. Gersix built only a few trucks during the war, and the industry languished. Like most manufacturing enterprises of the day, Gersix contributed to the war effort. Its repair shop was utilized, and its manufacturing facility produced a limited number of short-wheelbase trucks for the Japanese army, which fought against Germany in World War I.

After the armistice of November 1918, the robust Pacific Northwest economy, which had been stimulated by war production, began a sharp decline. Most of the 50,000 people employed by the region's shipbuilders during the war found themselves out of work, and many secondary businesses that had benefited from shipbuilding largesse folded. Regional employment dropped from a wartime peak of nearly 400,000 to just 75,000.

Government work, including long-delayed Federal Highway Act projects, helped reduce regional hardship and began to resuscitate the nearly suffocated truck manufacturing industry. Gersix trucks were now being built at a rate of four per month. As better components became available, new Gersix trucks were fitted with improved engines and five-speed transmissions. But they were still a far cry from modern-day trucks. Harry Hickey, a driver from that period, recalled that truckers "had to look out for brake fade. We had problems with the roads and hills and had to stay in low gear and often had smoking brakes at the bottom. On grades like that, many loggers would drag a log behind the truck as an extra brake. Any man who stayed in trucking in those early days was crazy."

2½ Ton Chassis

Complete with Starter and Electric Lights

F. O. B. Seattle
$2850

Specifications of
MODEL "G" GERSIX TRUCK

CAPACITY—5,000 lbs.
CHASSIS WEIGHT—5,000 lbs.
MOTOR—Buda: Six-Cylinder, Mono-Bloc, "L" Head Type, 3½-inch bore by 5¼-inch stroke.
MOTOR LUBRICATION—Force feed and splash.
HORSE POWER—Thirty, S. A. E. Rating.
CARBURETOR—Stromberg.
GAS CONTROL—Accelerator only.
GOVERNOR—Monarch.
IGNITION—Bosch High Tension Magneto.
STARTING MOTOR—Westinghouse: Bendix Drive.
BATTERY—Willard.
RADIATOR—Ideal: Cellular; cast aluminum tank type, mounted on side springs.
CLUTCH—Disc; Borg & Beck.
TRANSMISSION—Cotta: Mounted in unit with motor, selective individual clutch, three speeds forward and reverse. Gears always in mesh.
UNIVERSAL JOINTS—Blood.
DRIVE—Through three universal joints with self-aligning bearing in center.
REAR AXLE—Worm gear drive; full floating type; gear ratio 9 2/3 to 1.
FRONT AXLE—Liggett, 2¼x3½, "I" beam.
SPRINGS—Semi-elliptic, of special alloy steel; front 2¼x 42-inch; rear, 3x56-inch.

FRAME—Six-inch channel steel; cross-members riveted with heavy gusset plates; front spring supports riveted to side and cross-member; rigid construction.
WHEELS—36-inch wood, S. A. E. Standard.
TIRES—36x4 front; 36x7 rear.
STEERING GEAR—Ross irreversible, 18-inch wheel.
CONTROL—Steering gear on left; control levers in center.
WHEELBASE—150 inches.
TREAD—60 inches front and rear.
BEARINGS—Motor: Babbitt-lined bronze shells. Transmission and wheels; Bower roller bearings. Thrust bearing on worms and rear axle bearings; S. K. F. heavy duty.
GASOLINE CAPACITY—20 gallons.
BRAKES—Foot brake, 16x3-inch external contracting; hand brake, 16x3-inch internal expanding.
MAXIMUM BODY LENGTH—12 feet.
LOADING SPACE—Back of seat to end of frame, 132 inches.
EQUIPMENT—Electric side and tail lights, horn, oil can, jack and tool kit, Stewart vacuum system to feed gasoline to carburetor.
SPEED—Fifteen miles per hour.

THE GERSIX WARRANTY

WE warrant the motor trucks manufactured by us for one year after date of shipment to purchaser to be free from defects in material and workmanship and will furnish without charge, except for transportation, new parts in exchange for defective parts on their return to us at our factory, carriers' charges prepaid, if on inspection such parts are found by us to be defective. This warranty does not apply to tires and other trade accessories which are separately warranted by the manufacturers thereof.

This warranty is not binding on us if the failure of said parts is due to abnormal use, misuse, neglect or accident, or if the truck is loaded beyond its factory rated capacity, or if it is driven beyond its factory rated speed, or if the truck has been altered or repaired outside our factory without our written consent first obtained.

The manufacturer is not liable for conditions or obligations not herein expressed.

2319-23 Fifth Avenue   GERSIX MANUFACTURING CO.   Seattle, Washington

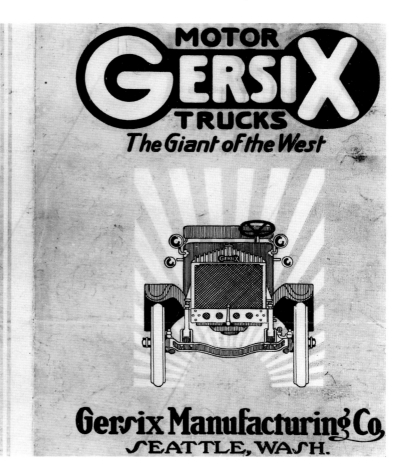

MOTOR GERSIX TRUCKS
The Giant of the West

Gersix Manufacturing Co.
SEATTLE, WASH.

GERSIX Truck Owned and Operated by Seattle Delivery & Transfer Co.

GERSIX Truck Operated by the Brooklyn Dairy, Seattle

GERSIX Truck Operating Between Seattle and Issaquah by Issaquah Freight Co.

GERSIX Truck Operated by the Whiton Hardware Co., Seattle

GERSIX Truck Owned and Operated by H. E. Tuck, at Kent, Wash.

A Western Truck for Western Work

The powerful **GERSIX** Motor Truck was brought on the market two years ago to meet the ever-increasing demand for a truck that could stand up under the extremely difficult road and hauling conditions of the Pacific Northwest.

About fifty per cent of the daily mileage of any Western truck is put in climbing hills, and over country roads with conditions most difficult, and a **specially designed** Western truck was the only solution to the hauling problem in many Northwestern industries. It was to meet these demands that the **GERSIX** Truck was designed.

Years of most careful study on the part of some of the best automobile engineers preceded the introduction of the **GERSIX**. This study revealed certain needs which are answered in the outstanding features of the **GERSIX**.

BEST FOR THE WEST

It was found that steady, even power was essential to the handling of heavy loads over rough loads. To avoid the constant changing of gears on rough roads, the SIX-CYLINDER engine was adopted as the standard of construction. Today this prove stands as the one big feature which has made the GERSIX unquestionably the BEST truck for use in the Pacific Northwest. Plenty of power to carry the heaviest load up the steepest hill, and smooth, evenly distributed power to carry heavy loads over rough roads at an economical speed without undue strains on the chassis and running gears, is given by the GERSIX sturdy SIX-CYLINDER motor and the worm gear drive.

At the very outset we set in to build a truck which would win a name for itself by the good work it did rather than by any claims that we could make for it, and this is just what has been accomplished.

BUILT FOR HEAVY WORK

THE GERSIX is built especially for heavy duty hauling. From the frame of six-inch channel steel to the special alloy steel springs, every rivet, every bolt, is made to withstand the wear and tear of the roughest roads, and the heaviest loads.

The power plant is equipped with select standard equipment, such as Bosch High Tension Magneto, Stromberg Carburetor, Westinghouse Electric Starting and Lighting System. The Transmission it exceptionally

Phantom View of GERSIX Trouble-Proof Transmission

serviceable, and is known as the Constant Mesh Type, the fact of the gears being in constant mesh eliminating the continual grinding and wear found in the sliding gears of other types of transmission.

The rear axle is Worm Driven, through oversize universal joints and propeller shafts carried on self-aligning bearings.

The load is carried on the Axle Housing, and the axle shafts are for driving only. The Differential may be taken out of the truck without disturbing the axle or wheels, or even removing the body.

Spring suspension has received the greatest attention, with the result that the GERSIX, with capacity load, rides like a touring car.

The Steering Device is of the best type that has been yet introduced—the Ross Irreversible—with the result that the car is always under control on the roughest roads and steers just as easy as the highest priced pleasure car.

MEETS HARDEST TESTS

The GERSIX stands today pre-eminently successful in the Pacific Northwest. Fully seventy-five per cent of the GERSIX trucks now in operation are daily subjected to the hardest use that a truck can be put to—hauling coal and wood, and being used in suburban auto freight runs.

NOTE THE HEAVY CONSTRUCTION OF THE GERSIX REAR END

SIDE VIEW SHOWING THE POWERFUL GERSIX MOTOR

One of two GERSIX Trucks Owned and Operated by the Ballard Transfer Company, Seattle

GERSIX Truck Owned and Operated by Taylor & Poynter, Seattle

GERSIX Truck Owned and Operated by Wainwright & McLeod, Seattle

GERSIX Truck Owned and Operated by the Puget Sound Coal Co., Seattle

GERSIX Truck Used in Construction Work by Cowlitz County Commissioners

1921 Gersix sales brochure.

FREDERICK KEEN RETIRED in 1919 and put his stake in Gersix up for sale. Edgar Worthington likely could have acquired Keen's share, but he left that opportunity to Harry W. Kent, not yet forty years old, who had been a partner with Worthington and Keen in Washington Tug and Barge. Kent was a prominent Seattle businessman with a background in shipbuilding: part owner and manager of Seattle Construction and Dry Dock Company, vice president and treasurer of Todd Dry Docks.

Kent and Worthington's business acumen figured prominently when it came to acquisitions. Gersix was one of four manufacturers of "Western trucks" in the Puget Sound area. Kent and Worthington considered mergers but decided that acquisitions made the most sense, buying out the parts and plans of two of their local competitors, HMR and Vulcan. In 1922 Gersix built and sold fifty-three trucks, most of them designed for general hauling within cities. Its line now included 1-ton, 2-ton, and 3-ton models.

The company began showing a profit. In December 1923, Worthington and Kent, along with company treasurer Theodore Jenner and office manager

Harry W. Kent (above) and Edgar Worthington. From their last names came the name of the Kenworth truck.

This fleet of
Kenworths is from
1923, the year the
Kenworth Motor
Truck Corporation
was founded.

At right, below:
Gersix and 1923
Kenworth name-
plate designs.

18

Adolph Engstrom, reincorporated as the Kenworth Motor Truck Corporation
—derived from the Kent and Worthington names—with $60,000 in
capital stock.

While the name changed, the company's business philosophy did not.
Kenworth continued to offer its customers custom-built trucks, though their
options were limited. The Buda four-cylinder engine was retained to power
the Kenworth, and improved pressed-steel frames were used instead of structural steel. Seven-speed transmissions and pneumatic tires were now available. Though cabs now had doors, side windows had not yet been added. The
company "didn't do much dilly-dallying" with its basic models, according
to Adolph Engstrom. "We were too busy trying to build a truck the way the
customer wanted. . . ."

CHAPTER TWO

MAKING THE SALE

Vernon Anthony Smith put Kenworth on the map. He would sell any truck his customers would buy, and then, as company pioneers recall, "He'd come back to the plant and say, 'Here, I have the sale, now we have to build them.' "

Smith was a legendary salesman who developed his talent in St. Louis at the Diamond T truck distributor. Following his first sale, eager to tell his boss of the success, he climbed behind the wheel of the old Cadillac truck he had taken in trade and started back to the office. Along the way, Smith totaled the truck; the customer had neglected to tell Smith about its broken steering gear. Red-faced but unhurt except in the pocketbook (he had to pay his employer for the loss), Smith was undaunted. He knew how to sell; he just needed practice in analyzing a good trade-in.

A few successful years later, Smith moved to Seattle to open his own Diamond T distributorship in 1916. In December 1922, Kenworth offered him a job as vice president and sales manager. He then dissolved the distributorship and went to work for Kenworth.

Selling for Kenworth provided a big advantage for a salesman: unlike other truck manufacturers, Kenworth offered attractive financing. And horse trading, in its literal sense, was in vogue, as was land trading. The adage "Anything to get the sale" became the implied message on Vernon Smith's calling card. He met customer needs for almost any type of truck: flatbeds, delivery trucks, dump trucks, even buses. And it worked. In 1924, Kenworth paid a dividend.

21

The 1920s saw many innovations in truck design. This early fleet illustrates the transition from solid to pneumatic tires and from open to enclosed cabs.

Page 20: 1929 Kenworth model 7 pump truck, powered by a Buda engine.

Previous page: Kenworth treasurer Theodore Jenner (left), sales manager Vernon Smith (center), and Seattle mayor Frank Edwards in 1929.

WHILE SELLING WAS SMITH'S FIRST LOVE, developing a regional distributor network for Kenworth was his future. In 1925 he established four dealerships in Washington state, mostly in small towns, and they began selling the two trucks a week produced at the Seattle plant. The basic Kenworth truck now included either a four-cylinder or a six-cylinder Buda engine, a seven-speed Brown-Lipe transmission, and a pressed-steel frame. But beyond such basic features, each Kenworth truck was unique, a customized model for a particular customer.

Smith often delivered truck orders to the factory along with specifications scribbled on scrap paper. Turning these Smith-scratchings into trucks was left to chief engineer John Holmstrom, whose mechanical genius contributed to Kenworth's early reputation for simplicity and for easy engine

access. Holmstrom had apprenticed at Kenworth as a floor-sweep, a mechanic's helper, and then a mechanic, work that paid for his engineering education at the University of Washington.

Old-fashioned gumption was second nature to Vernon Smith, a man who couldn't refuse a deal. "Everybody else was building standard stuff, and we were building anything that Vernon could sell," recalled company treasurer John Cannon. On several occasions, Smith wrote orders for small trucks (less than 1 ton), and the company lost money each time because it wasn't set up to manufacture small vehicles profitably. The Smith solution was to convince Diamond T to ship unassembled bodies of its smaller trucks to Seattle, where they were assembled and sold as the Kenworth model VS— the initials of the salesman himself.

KENWORTH COUNTERED THE COMPETITION from eastern manufacturers by touting the advantages of its trucks for use in the West. "A Western Truck for Western Work," its magazine ads would say. "About fifty percent of the daily mileage of any Western truck is put in climbing hills and over country roads with conditions most difficult."

Western trucks were engineered for western uses. The forests of the Pacific Northwest had been a cornerstone of the region's economy since the first mills were established along Puget Sound tidewater. At first, logs were cut along the shoreline and floated to local mills. As the fallers cut trees farther from waterways, railroads were built to carry the logs. As loggers moved even farther into mountain forests, roads were built and trucks were needed to haul logs to waterways or railheads. Trucks were also an economical solution for small logging companies that could not afford to build their own railroads.

The Kenworth legacy of trucks used in Pacific Northwest forests goes all the way back to the debut of that first solid-tired Gersix. But the company didn't offer a truck specifically designed for logging until 1928, when it produced the first model J for R. Malone of Ellensburg, Washington. It was the first logging truck of many that would eventually dominate Kenworth's order book.

British Columbia also represented potential sales for Kenworth, but import duties on completed trucks were prohibitive. Smith came up with a simple solution. Kenworth shipped unassembled trucks to Vancouver, where they were put together under the supervision of H. E. "Hank" Keifer. In November 1927, the first Canadian-made Kenworth was delivered. Expanding into Canada was a solid move, but selling trucks there was still a pioneering venture. When the Depression killed the market, Kenworth withdrew from international manufacturing.

WHEN HARRY KENT bought into the company that became Kenworth, he brought with him a system of cost accounting that he had learned in the shipbuilding business. It was new to Kenworth. Out went "build it and see if we make a profit," and in came "build it and know your margin." After that, the company rarely built anything at a loss.

Times were good for Kenworth and its eighty employees. The truck line now included ten models, all the way from 1 to 10 tons. Each truck featured electric starters, electric windshield wipers, and electric headlights as standard equipment. But with the company's growing success, the lack of manufactur-

A Giant Cedar Log

A mid-1920s Kenworth flatbed, equipped with bunks for hauling large logs, was typical of early logging trucks.

ing space at the Seattle plant became a problem, sometimes forcing operations onto the sidewalk. In summer, new trucks often were painted outdoors.

Office manager Adolph Engstrom was complaining that limited capital was holding Kenworth back. "We never had enough money," he said. "It was difficult to buy components in large quantities." Finally, in 1928, stockholders authorized an increase in capital stock from $60,000 to $300,000, mostly to support aggressive growth plans.

A new factory was paramount to Kenworth's future growth. The new plant had to be enormous—four times bigger than the old one. It would house manufacturing and the machine shop, executive offices, and an attractive showroom. The project was completed in May 1929. When Seattle mayor Frank Edwards officially opened the plant, the forecast was for a "sunny day and a bright future for Kenworth Motor Truck Corporation."

KENWORTH PROSPERED in the period before the Depression got its grip on the nation. Edgar Worthington retired from the company in 1929, and Kent succeeded him as president. Kenworth set up a new sales office in Portland. Air brakes and three-axle trucks were offered for the first time by Kenworth. And Vernon Smith continued his winning ways as he sold three dump trucks to the Department of Interior—a large order in its time.

All told, 1930 was another productive year for Kenworth, as 230 new trucks hit the road. But the region's economy was beginning to unwind as the Depression moved west. The following year, orders dropped by a third. When

27

Seattle mayor Frank Edwards cements a commemorative cornerstone on the new Kenworth factory at Yale and Mercer streets in 1929.

Previous pages:
Production work
proceeds in 1929 at
the Kenworth plant
at Yale and Mercer
streets in Seattle.

the company did sell a truck, the sale would often be followed by repossession when the owner couldn't meet payments. A new truck might have two or three lives in the hands of the repossessors before finding a permanent home.

In 1932 the company ceased to declare dividends. Now working with only a skeleton crew, Kenworth left its doors open, but just barely. The chance to service a truck was considered good business. Some of Kenworth's best Depression-era work was rebuilding older Kenworths for customers who couldn't afford new ones.

Hard times forced Smith to search further for new markets. From time to time, the truck company produced trailers to help make ends meet. About the only buyers for trucks were public agencies, fire departments, and bus companies. Fire chiefs each had their own idea of what was best on a truck, and Kenworth applied its custom-building experience to this profitable market. Kenworth engineer Jim Fitch became an expert on fire trucks, calling on regional fire departments and earning the nickname "Fire-Fighting" Fitch.

Kenworth went heavily into bus manufacture, which had been dominated by Heiser, Tricoach, and Wentworth & Irwin. Although Kenworth had built its first bus chassis in 1922 and a few more over the following decade, it wasn't until 1932 that buses became big business for the company.

Kenworth built a broad range of bus models, but the most innovative was a streamlined, all-steel coach. This deck-and-a-half bus with its center-mounted Hall Scott horizontal engine weighed 3,000 pounds less than its

This model 127 was designed and built for the Spokane, Washington, Fire Department in 1935.

30

competitors. It was purchased in large numbers by the North Coast Lines. At times during the Depression, bus manufacturing represented nearly a third of Kenworth's business.

Innovation, whether in seeking out new markets or developing new models, continued to strengthen Kenworth. The event that really made a

name for the company, though, was Kenworth's first factory installation of a diesel engine in a truck. Kenworth's retrofitting of gasoline-powered trucks with diesel engines proved the diesels to be both durable and economical at a time when diesel fuel was selling at just a third the price of gasoline.

Kenworth engineer Murray Aitken then drew up plans for a truck with a diesel engine as original equipment—the first such truck offered for sale by any manufacturer. Aitken's truck was powered by a 100-horsepower Cummins HA-4 diesel engine. The truck incorporated an important John Holmstrom idea: vent diesel exhaust straight up.

The company's chief engineer had driven a Kenworth retrofitted with a diesel engine, and he noted that any misadjustment of the engine's fuel injectors resulted in coal-black smoke. The smoke made it hard to see well enough to change lanes safely. So Holmstrom directed that diesel exhaust pipes be installed to rise vertically above the truck's cab. Kenworth's first order for a diesel-engine truck came from California-based Valley Motor Express Company. The company was so excited about the new vehicle that it requested the truck be shipped much of the way by water so that it would arrive truly "new."

31

As the diesel engine evolved, longer truck routes—Seattle to Los Angeles, Los Angeles to Chicago—were becoming commonplace. To help the long-haul truckers, Kenworth in 1933 became the first company to offer a sleeper cab. The sleeper had just enough room for a driver to lie down and catch a few hours of shut-eye.

The company's search for business during the Depression led to the creation of a wide network of distributorships. By 1937, Kenworth had dealers in eleven western states, the territories of Hawaii and Alaska, and Canada. One of its important early relationships was with the J. T. Jenkins Company, which represented Kenworth in California, Arizona, Texas, and New Mexico. Other dealerships included Roberts Motor Company in Portland, Oregon; Ferguson Truck and Equipment Company in Vancouver, British Columbia; Motor Power Equipment in Montana; and Von Hamm Young Company in Hawaii.

THE MOTOR CARRIER ACT of 1935, which fixed rates and routes and marked the beginning of federal regulation of the trucking industry, was a mixed blessing for truckers and for Kenworth. The independent nature of truckers and their industry had created bitter battles for territory, and the law gave regulatory power to the Interstate Commerce Commission. Regulations meant to bring stability to the trucking industry would remain in effect for the next half-century.

While Kenworth's customers welcomed the longer runs and increased revenue made possible by the 1935 Act, they also had to combat the problem of size and weight restrictions. Each state had its own standards

KENWORTH MOTOR TRUCKS
SERVE EVERY PURPOSE

Because of their dependability, efficiency, economy of operation and adaptability to every motor transportation requirement, we feature KENWORTH MOTOR TRUCKS. Sizes from 1 to 10-ton capacity, produced in one of the Northwest's most modern plants, and ideally suited to every hauling need of the territory which we serve. Your inspection of KENWORTH TRUCKS is cordially invited.

"Built Right in the West"

HOFIUS-FERRIS EQUIPMENT COMPANY
OFFICE AND WAREHOUSE 728-801 MALLON AVENUE,   SPOKANE, WASHINGTON

designed to protect bridges and highways. Kenworth engineers John Holmstrom, Bob Norrie, and others began testing lightweight aluminum components. Trucks with such components would be lighter and thus could haul a larger legal payload than those with all-steel construction. Despite scoffing from critics who said that aluminum would never work because it was too brittle, the company developed hubs, cabs, and bumpers of aluminum. The hubs, especially, proved so durable and became popular so quickly that competitors began offering them as well.

Holmstrom and his engineers followed up with more weight-saving and productivity improvements. They developed a six-wheel-drive truck model with hydraulic brakes, and a four-spring (bogie) suspension that became a calling card for Kenworth ingenuity. This innovation in truck suspension provided welcome relief for the backsides of many Kenworth drivers.

Challenges continued in 1936, when Kenworth's cab supplier, Heiser Body Works, closed its cab shop. Fortunately, ex-Heiser employees came to Kenworth and proposed that the company open its own cab shop. This new shop allowed Kenworth to develop its aluminum-working skills as it began building its own truck and bus cabs.

A 1937 Kenworth one-of-a-kind disaster truck. Carrying a wide range of equipment, it was prepared for emergencies ranging from fire fighting and first aid to cat rescues and food service.

THE DEPRESSION had reduced the fortunes of the rich and strained the nerves of the working class. Some of Kenworth's stockholders lost confidence in Harry Kent, and a struggle for control erupted. The unhappy stockholders went so far as hiring an accounting firm in an attempt to sniff out wrongdoing to bolster their case against Kent. Not about to give in, Kent asked Philip Johnson to buy into the company. Johnson had been forced out as president of Boeing and United Airlines, largely because of the Government's cancellation of airmail delivery contracts and an antitrust suit against the parent firm of the two companies. In 1936, Johnson bought the stock of Kent's detractors, gaining control of about 25 percent of Kenworth.

Kent and Johnson reshaped the Kenworth board with new directors and company officers, including themselves and Seattle businessman and investor Frederick Fisher. Kent continued as president, while Johnson became first vice president. Vernon Smith and John Holmstrom were second and third vice presidents, respectively.

Johnson had just joined the company when its employees went out on strike. Depression-era labor was restless, and Kenworth's general manager,

36

Ray Hinea, had initiated a piecework system of payment that seemed logical but worked poorly. For starters, there wasn't enough work to go around. And if repairs to a job were needed, the cost came out of the worker's own pocket. Kenworth employees struck in February 1936, Seattle Teamsters refused pickups and deliveries, and the plant was shut down.

Fortunately for Kent, Johnson was more than just an idle investor. A talented labor administrator, Johnson resolved employee concerns in a few days. He eliminated the piecework pay system (along with the manager who had implemented it) and increased wages to $1 per hour—big pay for that time (across town, Boeing was paying only 60 cents per hour). Kenworth employees were given two weeks of annual paid vacation and, later, a five-day work week.

Johnson's heart still belonged to the aviation industry, and in August 1936 he began a slow departure from Kenworth as he helped establish Trans-Canada Airlines, splitting his time between the two companies. Two months later, Harry Kent died. Johnson became president of Kenworth, and he appointed Adolph Engstrom as the company's vice president and general manager.

WITH THE STRIKE and stockholder strife behind it, Kenworth once again focused full attention on selling and building trucks. Smith's search for new markets continued to take him far from Kenworth's home. On a

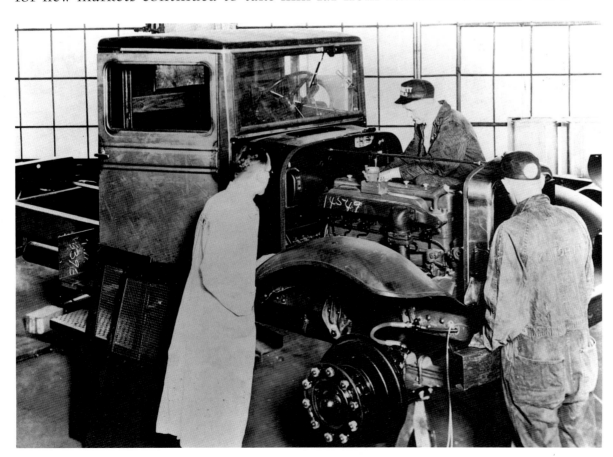

A Kenworth engineer supervises the manufacture of a Kenworth truck in the mid-1930s.

sales trip to Hawaii, he watched sugarcane being hauled by rail over temporary tracks laid in muddy fields. He approached the sugar companies with an
offer to build trucks designed for field conditions, and returned to Seattle
with a pocket full of orders for gas-powered, six-wheel-drive cane trucks.
(Within ten years, Kenworth trucks were in use on thirteen of Hawaii's four-
teen sugar plantations.)

   Later in 1936, Kenworth engineers created the model 520, the first
cab-over-engine (COE) truck, whose design was spurred by federal and state
requirements for shorter overall tractor-trailer lengths. This cab-over-engine
(COE) truck, referred to by some as the "bubble-nose," met New Mexico's
strict limitation on total weight per axle and its length limit of 45 feet. The
model 520 proved aerodynamically superior to any truck cab on the road,

but its unconventional look was not readily accepted by drivers. It was ahead of its time and an oddity on the highway.

With the Depression nearing an end in 1937, Holmstrom led his engineers on a quest for innovations. Building on a design theory first discussed over a late-night dinner, they created what became known as a rear-axle, torsion-bar suspension that reduced truck weight by using a steel bar in place of a heavy leaf spring.

Smith and Holmstrom were the "doers" at Kenworth—getting the orders, then designing and building the trucks just the way the customer wanted. They helped lead Kenworth through the Depression years with many innovations, from custom fire trucks and buses to sleepers and diesel-powered trucks.

CHAPTER THREE

MUDDY BOOTS

*Philip Johnson saw the future of Kenworth in its engineering and manufac-
turing prowess. To make the company's plant more conducive to great work,
Johnson told Kenworth management to "figure out what you need and we'll
find a way to get it." Then the company issued preferred stock in the
amount of $700,000 to pay for Johnson's vision.*

41

*This kind of progressive thinking was just what the company needed.
The Depression had been difficult for Kenworth. When Johnson invested in
the company in 1936, its plant was run-down and machinery was in disre-
pair. Kenworth's production rate had declined, and employee morale was low.
Capital from the stock sale enabled the company to retire its bank debt and
renovate its aging plant.*

*Johnson believed that to be competitive, Kenworth would always need
first-rate engineers. The John Holmstrom–led engineering staff at Kenworth
became known as the Seven BSMEs (for their academic degree, bachelor of
science in mechanical engineering). They represented engineering inventive-
ness unmatched by other manufacturers in the region. They included Murray
Aitken and Les Dafoe, who designed buses; Bob Norrie, who specialized in
highway trucks; John Czarniecki and Wally Brown, who made up the team
usually assigned to special-purpose trucks sold by Vernon Smith; and Jim
Fitch and Al McLean, the company's fire-truck specialists.*

"THIS GROUP WAS VERY CAPABLE and always able to rise to the occasion," Czarniecki recalled. "No matter what the problem, we could still solve it. I think it was because we had an open mind and were willing to talk to each other." It was a social group as well, with the men often visiting each other's homes, playing golf, or going dancing together with their wives. "If we had to work on a Saturday or Sunday or after work, we got together and did it—we didn't worry about getting paid for it," said Czarniecki. "We did things to help each other out for the company's sake; we were company men."

42

Page 40: Front-wheel differential case and underbelly of a 1930s sugar-cane hauler. This grill design, which became known as the shovel nose, was the genesis of modern Kenworth grills.

Previous page: Development and manufacturing of military trucks consumed most of Kenworth's capacity shortly after the start of World War II.

MANY TRUCK AND BUS MODELS represented innovations unique to Kenworth. The company built twenty-one-passenger convertible sightseeing buses for the Mount Rainier National Park Company, a streamlined cab-over-engine (COE) fire truck for MGM Studios, and trucks with aerated and temperature-controlled tanks for hauling spawning salmon around dams on the Columbia River. Kenworth engineers also continued work on more "traditional" projects, developing the first of the company's "Big Loggers"— model numbers 548, 549, and 550—featuring heavy-duty frame-rails with four-wheel-drive power.

By the late 1930s, Kenworth engineers had earned a reputation for solving problems in the field, often driving trucks or inspecting them in the middle of a muddy road for signs of failure. Their motto was "Kenworth engineers wear muddy boots." Holmstrom would routinely visit logging sites, crawling under vehicles and making notes on how to improve truck design to

43

better withstand the rugged conditions. Aitken drove bus routes with
Canadian Greyhound to get a feel for the environment in which buses worked
and to seek ways to improve their ride, comfort, and durability. Engineer
Al McLean was often spotted behind the wheel of a fire truck.

Not all innovations proved successful. Trying to take weight savings to
the next level, Kenworth worked with the Cummins Engine Company to
develop an all-aluminum engine block. The savings in weight was definitely
there, but durability was not. Thousands of miles of testing demonstrated
that the block could not live up to its promise, and the project was scrapped.

Throughout the late 1930s and early 1940s, it became common to
build a sleeper into the front end of the trailer. These "sleeper-in-nose
trailers" were popular with drivers because of their comfort and headroom,
although the loss of cargo space in the 32-foot trailers was a drawback.
There were also safety concerns: the person in the sleeper had no contact
with the driver, and the sleeper offered little protection in case of an accident. In addition, daredevil drivers would climb from the sleeper in the
trailer up to the cab while the truck was moving down the highway. (The
sleeper-in-nose trailer was eventually banned, in 1952, by the Department
of Motor Carrier Safety.)

1936 21-passenger
Canadian
Greyhound bus.

46

Kenworth engineers were good listeners, and drivers commonly gave them their two cents worth. In her 1973 book *Relics of the Road*, Gini Rice recounted how a driver making Seattle–to–Los Angeles runs complained long and hard that the ride in his trailer's sleeper compartment was so rough it was "killing" him. Kenworth already offered an integrated sleeper as a possible solution, but this driver wanted something altogether new: a separate sleeping area. Kenworth engineer Bob Dickey developed a modular sleeper— a separate sleeping compartment with an opening, protected by a rubber gasket, connecting to the cab. The driver was so happy with the sleeper that he stopped by the Kenworth plant to offer his thanks. "But you should have given this to me for free," he added. "Everywhere I go, people ask me, 'Where did you get that?' "

By the end of the 1930s, Kenworth trucks were selling in a wide price range, from $2,500 to $16,500. Company dividends, suspended during much of the Depression, were again being paid to stockholders. And with money generated from its sale of stock, the company was debt free and well equipped.

Philip Johnson had proven his talents to Kenworth, but he also had proven his management ability in the aviation industry, first at Boeing and United Airlines, then at Trans-Canada Airlines. In 1939, he again accepted the presidency of Boeing—but he also remained as president of Kenworth. Adolph Engstrom continued as vice president and general manager.

THINGS WERE GOING WELL for Kenworth, but clouds of war were

gathering. World political tension was high. The Axis powers were on the march, and the United States began preparing for the war that everyone knew would come. Kenworth had 250 people on its payroll, and truck production was in overdrive. By the time the Japanese attacked the U.S. naval base at Pearl Harbor on December 7, 1941, Kenworth was also producing parts for the Boeing B-17 Flying Fortress. Most of its commercial truck production was converted to war machinery manufacturing.

With its well-equipped factory and skilled employees, Kenworth was given an A-3 defense priority rating, the highest for a vehicle manufacturer not directly involved in defense contracts. But Kenworth recognized that in order to survive the wartime economy, it would have to compete for defense

B-17s on the Boeing Company airfield. Kenworth saw much of its truck manufacturing converted to the military effort in World War II, including manufacture of subassemblies for B-17s.

contracts. Holmstrom traveled to Washington, D.C., and returned with an Army contract to build 430 four-ton, six-wheel-drive M-1 Wreckers.

The Wrecker was a hybrid truck, customized for extreme duty and heavy lifting. A crane mounted on its chassis had fore and aft winches for retrieving tanks from deep mud or shell holes. The truck also came with cutting and welding equipment for the field repair of tanks and other rolling stock. The design of the Wrecker incorporated the Kenworth innovations that had gone into its sugarcane-hauling trucks.

Late in 1942, orders for 1,500 more Wreckers taxed the capacity of the Seattle plant. Taking a cue from the automobile industry, Kenworth built a moving production line, replacing its traditional stall-built method of manufacture. Other production jockeying took place as three sub-plants were established. A new repair and service shop was opened to help keep civilian trucks on the road. In that first year of war production, Kenworth built 232 military and 166 commercial units.

In 1943, Seattle was designated by the War Department as a critical labor area, with priority given to airplane manufacture and shipbuilding. If Kenworth wanted to keep its defense contracts, it would have to move its manufacturing out of the area. Engstrom estimated it would cost the company more than $10 million in government contracts if the company did not make the move. So Kenworth set up a temporary factory in buildings on the county fairgrounds in Yakima, Washington, about 150 miles southeast of Seattle. With the move—and perhaps as a sign of good faith—the War Production Board gave Kenworth an order for 800 five-ton 4x2 vehicles for Army Ordnance.

Labor was still a critical problem, even in Yakima, where most workers' experience was in farming. But they all knew how to repair equipment, and plant superintendent Hank Keifer found they could build trucks as well. Despite all the commotion involved in moving a manufacturing plant and training new employees, Kenworth was able to produce 709 military vehicles, plus a smattering of commercial vehicles for uses on the "civilian war front."

Similar to the rugged Kenworth cane haulers developed during the 1930s, the six-wheel-drive M-1 Wrecker was developed for the U.S. Army and manufactured in 1942.

Back in Seattle, the main Kenworth plant and seven smaller locations were set up to support manufacture of the Boeing B-17 Flying Fortress and B-29 Super Fortress. The main plant at Yale and Mercer streets was still turning out a few civilian trucks, so a fence was erected down the middle of the facility to keep the work for Boeing completely separate from areas designated for work on trucks, as required by government security.

Three shifts of workers carried out subassembly work on the planes' nose sections, bomb bay doors, and bulkheads. Of Kenworth's 507 Seattle employees, 415 were women. "These women came out from behind kitchen sinks and didn't know how to hold a screwdriver," engineer Czarniecki said. "We had a training program in the basement of the old plant. As soon as the women could use that screwdriver, we brought them upstairs and put them on production work." Czarniecki had high praise for the women: "They won the war for us."

There was no time to rest during the war years, as Kenworth's overall employment jumped to 800. In 1944, truck production at Yakima totaled 716 military vehicles and 217 commercial units, while an untold number of aircraft parts and subassemblies were produced in Seattle.

The M-1 Wreckers performed as well overseas as Kenworth trucks did in the rugged backwoods of the Pacific Northwest. Sergeant Carl Christofferson of the 780th Amphibious Tank Battalion described an experience with one of the Wreckers late in the war: "The real test came in actual combat when, after 40 days at sea, it was put aground in the Philippine

Islands on A-Day, October 20, 1944. Day after day through sticky mud, which covered the tops of the wheels, our Kenworth toiled—recovering tanks from shell holes under Japanese mortar fire, keeping traffic moving along almost impossible roads, and fording rivers with water at the driver's feet..."

TWO OF KENWORTH'S LEADERS would not live to see the end of the war. Just months apart in 1944 came the deaths of Frederick Fisher, a company director, and company president Philip Johnson. Johnson was only 49, a man widely admired for his enterprising leadership in the aviation and trucking industries.

Engstrom had managed the company's day-to-day operations and continued to direct its momentum. But with the earlier death of Kent and now the deaths of Johnson and Fisher, their widows became the majority owners of Kenworth. They offered to sell their stock to Engstrom, Holmstrom, and other company employees. But because of wartime work and the company's promising future, Kenworth's value now exceeded the financial resources of the group.

This opened the door for another Puget Sound business visionary, Paul Pigott, who was president of and a major stockholder in Pacific Car and Foundry, a rail-car manufacturer based in Renton, Washington. Pigott also

Philip Johnson
served as president
of both Kenworth
and the Boeing
Company until his
death in 1944.

owned a significant interest in the Everett Pacific Company, a wartime shipyard in Everett, Washington, and held a stock interest in Standard Oil of
California. When he was offered the chance to buy the heirs' majority stock
in Kenworth, he wasted no time in making the acquisition.

Pigott was very much aware of Kenworth's potential. Pacific Car had
often competed with Kenworth for bus contracts. When Seattle's bus
manufacturing shops were closing, it was Pacific Car that had acquired both
Heiser and Tricoach. And while Kenworth was producing M-1 Wreckers
in Yakima, Pacific Car was producing M-26 tank retrievers in Billings,
Montana. The company was also building Sherman tanks in its Renton
plant. To Pigott, Kenworth and Pacific Car seemed a perfect fit.

Pigott became Kenworth's president. Ferdinand Schmitz, with Pacific
Car since 1937, was elected vice president. Vernon Smith remained with the
company as vice president and chief salesman, while John Holmstrom was
named Kenworth's vice president and general manager to succeed Engstrom,
who resigned following his failed attempt to acquire the company.

"Paul Pigott not only recognized Kenworth's potential," wrote Alex
Groner in *PACCAR: The Pursuit of Quality*, "but he was aware that Johnson
had been the moving force behind the company and he took on the
responsibility of filling that void himself. Like Johnson, he was completely
in accord with the Kenworth ideas of custom truck building and engineering
innovation."

Following pages:
At war's end,
Kenworth resumed
its sales efforts,
including its inter-
est in the Hawaiian
sugarcane truck
market.

51

ON A ROLL

The purchase of Kenworth in 1944 by Pacific Car and Foundry couldn't have come at a better time for the truck company or its new parents. Truck building was shifting from military to commercial markets, and pent-up demand would mean new and large orders. Kenworth raced to develop new technology and to expand its network of dealers.

The transition in ownership had been smooth. Kenworth was operated as a wholly owned subsidiary of Pacific Car and Foundry and remained mostly autonomous. Paul Pigott encouraged progressive thinking, new materials, and new manufacturing methods. Kenworth engineers found his direction clear but challenging.

As the war came to an end, defense contracts were being canceled. The three production lines of Kenworth's B-17 parts came to a halt. The company that had produced more than 2,100 trucks for the military made a rapid transition into peacetime trucks for commercial uses. One of the first orders was a government contract for trucks to be used in the reconstruction of Europe. For this fleet, Kenworth used leftover war materiel. During that first postwar year, 50 percent of all Kenworth trucks produced were destined for France, the Netherlands, or Belgium.

MANY PEOPLE FEARED A POSTWAR RECESSION similar to the one that followed World War I, but it never happened. During World War II it had been nearly impossible to buy a new truck, and those on the road were well past their life expectancy. Kenworth knew it was just a matter of time before civilian truck buyers would be back knocking at Vernon Smith's door.

"We are going to be ready with manufacturing facilities far in advance of any others west of the Mississippi," Pigott proclaimed. Like Philip Johnson, his predecessor as president, Pigott planned to invest in the company's plant.

In October 1945, Kenworth purchased the former Fisher Body Plant, a 13-acre facility on East Marginal Way in south Seattle (which was increased to 26 acres in the 1960s). "Now we have the plant we've always wanted and needed," general manager John Holmstrom said. "As soon as the material supply situation clears up, there'll be no stopping us."

More than trucks, Kenworth engineers created new manufacturing systems. The new plant, with four times the capacity of Kenworth's prewar facilities, included a chain conveyor production line that extended the length of the structure. The first truck rolled off the line on March 3, 1946, far ahead of the plant's full completion. Scarcity of parts and a plant only partially built meant that truck building proceeded slowly, and bus production slower yet. The wartime Yakima facility helped in the transition to the new plant by continuing to build trucks until the end of April 1946.

Kenworth's East Marginal Way plant in 1946.

Orders for new trucks began pouring in from Smith and the sixteen Kenworth dealerships in the Pacific and southwestern states and the eighteen dealers in South America. By the end of 1946, 705 trucks had been produced—but more than 2,000 orders were declined because the new plant simply couldn't handle all the work.

With the order book showing a $12 million backlog, the times were literally too good to be true. In sorting through company paperwork, treasurer John Cannon became suspicious that some orders weren't worth the paper they were written on.

"We had all these orders, and we were ordering all these parts, but I couldn't see how these trucks would ever be paid for," Cannon said. "The dealers didn't have the money, and we didn't have the money or the capital available to finance them, and the banks were only handling them on a truck-by-truck basis." Cannon and Pigott concluded that an order audit was necessary. By the end of the first week of audits, 1,000 orders had to be canceled. Cannon then created an order-taking procedure that reduced the danger of any more orders being placed before a buyer's credit was approved.

Kenworth was offering its customers commercial models ranging from a supercharged oil hauler to heavy-duty logging and dump trucks. The giant of the line, model 888, was a chain-drive vehicle with a gross vehicle weight of up to 110,000 pounds, built for construction or logging. The truck featured double back-to-back frame rails, whereas standard trucks used only one set. Loggers took full advantage of this off-road workhorse, often stacking it with as many logs as the 16-foot bunks could possibly hold.

Its development interrupted by World War II, the innovative torsion-bar suspension became standard equipment on Kenworth trucks by 1950.

By 1950 Kenworth offered 27 models. New designs were bolstered by innovations such as torsion-bar suspension, which had been placed on hold during the war. Experience in manufacturing aluminum components paid off, resulting in an extruded-aluminum truck frame offering tremendous weight savings.

One of the most unusual new models was a 40-foot snowplow vehicle built for the state of Alaska and designed to clear the road from the oil port of Valdez to the inland town of Fairbanks—a distance of 366 miles.

57

Kenworth developed a heavyweight truck matched to Alaska's extreme weather. The truck needed to be heavy enough to drive a wide plow. Kenworth's solution was to load the bed with rocks, coat them with water, and then repeat the process several times. The frozen water added weight, and soon the truck tipped the scales at more than 50 tons.

DETERMINED TO DEVELOP international markets, Pigott sent John Holmstrom on a trip to South America, Africa, and the Middle East. Among the orders produced was a contract for fifty buses for Uruguay.

Pigott also promoted Kenworth's image as a custom truck builder. "As you become known, and as your engineers gain experience that perhaps no other organization can match, you're called in more and more on special transportation problems," Pigott said in a 1948 article in *Business Week*. "We are never through with diversification as long as there is a need for products which our engineers can develop and which our plants can turn out."

Thanks to Kenworth's reputation for innovation and to insights Pigott gained as a member of the board of Standard Oil of California, Kenworth got an order in 1947 to design and build special-purpose trucks for the Arabian American Oil Company (ARAMCO). These trucks had to withstand air temperatures of up to 135 degrees Fahrenheit. But the most difficult engineering challenge was to design a truck with superior traction that could haul heavy payloads over the bottomless sands of Saudi Arabia. The result was the model 853. With a 64,000-pound capacity, the truck featured side-by-side radiators, six-wheel drive, a fuel capacity of 300 gallons, and a 318-horsepower Hall Scott gasoline engine.

Working with Goodyear Tire engineers, Kenworth specified a new tire for the model 853—a low-pressure balloon-type model for use in sand. To calculate the optimum weight-to-surface ratio, engineers measured a camel's hoofprint and then weighed the camel. This became the truck's per-square-inch weight distribution. Kenworth tested its camel theory on the sand dunes near Yuma, Arizona. It worked, and an initial shipment of sixteen trucks was on its way to the Middle East. The balance of the order—twenty-six trucks, along with parts—was shipped three months later. Kenworth stationed customer service representatives in Saudi Arabia, where the trucks were used in building the Trans-Arabian Pipeline, then the world's largest construction project.

Following the success of the model 853, Kenworth also developed smaller trucks for ARAMCO. By 1949, international sales represented more than 40 percent of the company's business. And through the late 1940s and 1950s, ARAMCO was Kenworth's largest customer, ordering well over 1,000 units.

TO HELP PROPEL Kenworth's bus division, the company hired H. E. Simi, a nationally recognized bus designer. He helped the company develop lightweight metal buses and trackless trolleys with streamlined contours. The city of Portland, Oregon, was one of the first to take notice, quickly putting in an order for 50 trackless trolleys.

One of the buses produced at Kenworth was an odd-looking creation called the Bruck—half bus and half truck. The Bruck, made to order for Northern Pacific Transport Company, was the brainchild of Kenny Allen of Motor Power Equipment, Kenworth's distributor in Billings, Montana, with help from the superintendent of Northern Pacific. The idea was passed on to Kenworth engineers, who produced the final design.

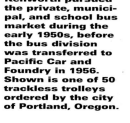

Kenworth pursued the private, municipal, and school bus market during the early 1950s, before the bus division was transferred to Pacific Car and Foundry in 1956. Shown is one of 50 trackless trolleys ordered by the city of Portland, Oregon.

63

Produced in the 1950s, the Bruck—half bus, half truck—represented an engineering solution for the mixed needs of Northern Pacific Transport Company.

"Northern was shutting down rail lines in Montana but was still obligated to carry people and freight," recalled Moe Buringrud, a longtime Kenworth executive and engineer. "They needed a vehicle that could do both, so they came up with the Bruck concept. Its front section was built like a school bus, with room for seventeen passengers, and the rear was an 18-foot van that carried freight."

Although the Bruck never caught on outside Montana, several were built over the two-year life of the program. In 1951, Great Northern

Opposite: ARAMCO became one of Kenworth's largest customers, ordering more than 1,700 trucks by 1960. Shown is a 1953 model 853 destined for the Middle East.

Previous pages: In 1949, international sales for models including trucks for the Arabian American Oil Company (ARAMCO) accounted for more than 40 percent of Kenworth's business.

Transport ordered a larger version of the vehicle, with room for twenty-one passengers and 7 tons of freight. It was one of the last bus orders Kenworth would ever accept. Bus production, much of it stall-built, interfered with truck production. Bus building was regional, with most orders coming from the West Coast and the mountain states. Truck orders, on the other hand, were fast-developing in the eastern United States. The bus division was transferred back to Pacific Car and Foundry in 1956, eventually to be broken up into municipal and school units and ultimately sold to other companies.

In the early 1950s, Kenworth and Boeing experimented with gas-turbine-powered trucks.

KENWORTH'S EARLY TIES with Boeing through Philip Johnson, along with the company's subsequent work on the B-17 and B-29 warplanes, gave Kenworth engineers a close relationship with their counterparts at Boeing. In 1950 Boeing, under a U.S. Navy contract to develop a gas turbine engine, had come up with a 175-horsepower engine that proved to be clean, light, and powerful. Boeing suggested that Kenworth explore the use of turbine-powered engines for trucks.

A 200-pound gas turbine was fitted into a conventional Kenworth truck, taking up only 13 percent of the space required by an equally powerful 2,700-pound diesel engine. The truck was test-driven from Canada to Mexico, its hood locked down to maintain secrecy and security. Kenworth also worked with West Coast Fast Freight of Seattle on test runs from Seattle to Los Angeles.

The turbine engine had problems. The Seattle–Los Angeles run was taking four or five hours longer than usual. The turbine-equipped truck put out too much exhaust, had poor acceleration, and was tough on clutches. Fuel economy, or lack of it, was another problem: the truck traveled only 1 mile per gallon. The project was scrapped.

Disappointment for engineers at Kenworth never lasted long, because new projects were always on the horizon. With the Korean War, military development and production once again became a significant part of Kenworth's business. The company manufactured sixty-seven highly specialized vehicles called T-10 transporters, designed to move 35-ton, 280-millimeter "atomic cannons"—the world's first weapon capable of firing an atomic shell. It took two T-10s to transport one cannon, which was mounted on a cradle with a truck positioned at either end. Each T-10 unit was independently driven, and drivers communicated via intercom to coordinate steering.

The entire unit—more than 84 feet long and weighing 170,000 tons—was Kenworth's largest vehicle to date. Powered by 375-horsepower air-cooled engines, the T-10s featured four-wheel drive and had a top speed of 35 miles per hour. The units were nimble enough to maneuver around a 28-foot street corner. The cannon could be positioned, raised, fired, and moved within ten minutes. The cannon and its transport vehicles were showcased to the world at President Dwight Eisenhower's inaugural parade in 1953.

Two identical Kenworths, the gas-turbine-powered truck on the left and a conventional diesel on the right.

65

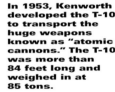

In 1953, Kenworth developed the T-10 to transport the huge weapons known as "atomic cannons." The T-10 was more than 84 feet long and weighed in at 85 tons.

A GROWING NETWORK of dealers was at work moving the Kenworth truck line. Penetration of the logging truck market was due in part to Roberts Motor Company, Kenworth's oldest dealership. Founder O. W. Roberts sold a variety of truck brands—Wilcox Trux, Republic, Federal, and finally Faogel—before taking on the Kenworth line in 1938. Over the years the business in Portland expanded to include locations in Medford and Eugene, Oregon, and in Redding and Eureka, California, as it sold thousands of Kenworth logging trucks.

Kenworth customers sometimes became Kenworth dealers. That was the recipe for at least two longtime dealers, Kenworth Sales in Salt Lake City, Utah, and Williams Equipment Sales in Spokane, Washington. The Salt Lake City operation got under way following a discussion between Vernon Smith and Walter Jay Treadway, a veteran driver and manager for Garrett Freight Lines.

"You know our trucks so well," Smith said, "why don't you sell them?" Treadway's son Gene recalled that his father gave Smith's question a lot of thought. "He didn't think he could sell," Gene Treadway said. "But he was a natural because he had experience in the trucking business. He could tell people whether they'd make money on what they were going to haul. And he could tell them how to do it."

Walter Jay Treadway opened his Salt Lake City dealership in 1945, and sold twenty trucks the first year. The end of World War II brought a demand for trucks from operators who had cash and no trades, spurring tremendous growth for the business. The dealership later expanded to locations in Nevada and Idaho, plus a partnership with Hatch Barrett and his Trebar Kenworth operation in Idaho.

"Kenworth was considered the Cadillac of trucks," Gene Treadway observed. "We had one service station guy in town that would let you charge fuel if you rolled up in a Kenworth. If you didn't have a KW, you paid cash. That's just the way it was in those days."

In 1945, Vernon Smith also had his eye on another potential dealer, Roy Williams—sales manager for Spokane's Inland Empire Refining Company, a Kenworth customer. Williams returned home from a visit to the Kenworth factory and decided to open what was to become the company's fifth dealership.

"Our first store wasn't big, but it did house parts, a sales office, and room for one truck to hide out from the rain," recalled Neal Williams, who took over the dealership from his father in 1967.

The market in the early days was primarily logging trucks and some tankers. Success later brought expansion within Washington and into Idaho and Montana. Sales continued to be dominated by logging trucks and the occasional off-highway vehicle for work on Columbia River hydroelectric projects until the completion of Interstate 90 in the late 1960s. Spokane suddenly became a thoroughfare for general freight trucks, and sales of over-the-road trucks became the order of the day.

Sold through Rihm Motor Company, Kenworth's St. Paul, Minnesota, dealer, this 200-horsepower model 523 bullnose had an overall length of 45 feet. It was designed for heavy hauling between eastern coal fields and Minnesota's iron mines.

67

KENWORTH BROKE ALL production records in 1952, turning out more than 1,000 trucks. It seems fitting that Kenworth hit that landmark the same year Vernon Smith retired, after thirty years as sales manager and vice president. Smith's legacy included a solid network of distributors—who showed their appreciation to Smith with a retirement gift of a new Cadillac. Only a few people worked at Kenworth when Smith began his spectacular sales career there, but employment topped 1,000 by the time he retired.

Smith retired from a booming trucking industry. Urban sprawl and the decline of railroads resulted in trucks carrying a growing percentage of all land-moved freight, increasing from 173 billion ton-miles in 1950 to 223 billion ton-miles by 1955 and representing 17.5 percent of all land-moved freight. Kenworth was making significant inroads into the truck market in the midwestern and eastern United States, partly on the strength of its experience in building vehicles with lightweight components.

With new dealerships and customers farther away from the West Coast, Kenworth set up a 6,000-square-foot parts warehouse in Chicago in 1953. It was quickly outgrown. In 1955, the company built a 25,000-square-foot Chicago warehouse, sharing it with Pacific Car and Foundry. Soon it was necessary to use 50,000 square feet, and then 100,000. During this period, Kenworth put all its standard parts information and service manuals onto microfilm, giving dealers a complete and convenient parts record of every truck.

One of the first Kenworth trucks to meet with success in the Midwest was a radical new design: a cab-beside-engine (CBE) model developed in response to a request for improved visibility.

Bob Norrie, then chief engineer, recalled that Kenworth started on the new design "with the requirements for ideal visibility and no preconceived ideas for how the finished truck should look. Our first thought in making every decision was its effect upon the driver's view of the road."

"This is just like flying a plane!" was the reaction from one driver who tried the new truck and then persuaded his boss to order several of the unusual-looking vehicles. By eliminating the passenger area and replacing it with a canvas seat for a second person behind the driver, Kenworth did more than improve visibility. It cut more than 1,000 pounds from the truck's weight, allowing more cargo for companies such as Yellow Transit Freight Lines of Kansas City, which ordered 300 of the trucks. Other companies followed suit, and for two years the truck enjoyed a prominent place on Kenworth's order board.

"There was driver opposition to it," recalled Don Grimes, who was a Kenworth sales executive. "Some drivers feared for their safety in case of an accident because they felt the truck didn't give the protection of a full-fledged

69

cabover." But even with the opposition to the cab-beside-engine (CBE) design in 1955, the cyclical truck market bounced up 75 percent from the year before, as Kenworth built 1,505 units.

NORTH OF THE BORDER, Kenworth opened a manufacturing plant in Burnaby, British Columbia, next to the city of Vancouver, also in 1955. Canada had imposed a high tariff on truck imports to help protect its manufacturers. The tariff crippled Kenworth's Canadian distributor, Ferguson Truck and Equipment Company, which encouraged Kenworth to counter the tariff by building trucks in Canada.

"Initially, it was almost all logging trucks," according to Donald Pennell, who managed the new plant. Kenworth redesigned existing models especially for the Canadian logging industry, which was moving toward larger and larger trucks. "But Canada had just begun its massive highway expansion, and the demand for highway trucks was growing. We developed the highway-truck market once we were there." After only one year, Kenworth outsold Hayes Manufacturing, its principal Canadian competitor. (In 1974, Hayes was purchased by Canadian Kenworth.)

Kenworth had a reputation in Canada and elsewhere for developing heavy-duty trucks that met customer needs. Demand for large-capacity

earthmovers was strong, going well beyond the 12-cubic-yard model 801 the company had introduced. So Kenworth developed two super-size trucks in 1955, models 802-B and 803. The 802-B was a truck-tractor with a dump semitrailer able to pack up to 32 cubic yards. The 803 was probably the largest two-axle earthmoving truck in existence, with a capacity of 28 cubic yards.

A large order from Pacific Intermountain Express in 1955 created a new freight model, the 844. Three variations of the 844 evolved, with the most unusual featuring special air suspension springs, two sets of front wheels on tandem axles for steering, a large cargo box (called a dromedary) between the cab and the fifth-wheel coupling, and a horizontal Cummins engine under the frame in back of the cab.

As business continued to grow, Kenworth Motor Truck Corporation officially became a division of Pacific Car and Foundry. Effective September 12, 1955, it was the Kenworth Motor Truck Company. The Interstate and Defense Highway Act later that year authorized construction of thousands of miles of new roadways in the United States. It was another affirmation that Pacific Car, Kenworth, and the trucking industry were on a roll.

CHAPTER FIVE

THE WORLD OF KENWORTH

The global history of Kenworth would certainly have been far different had it not been for the original 1947 order from the Arabian American Oil Company (ARAMCO) for a new breed of desert-climate, off-road truck. The order for twenty-six trucks gave Kenworth and parent company Pacific Car and Foundry (PACCAR) a foothold in a new part of the world. "It showcased Kenworth's abilities and made us world-renowned for making large, durable trucks," said Gabriel Pepino, president of PACCAR International. Kenworth now had a line of tough desert trucks hauling huge oil rigs across the desert. More orders came in from Saudi Arabia, Sudan, Abu Dhabi, and eventually China.

Kenworth was quick to capitalize on its growing reputation in the Middle East. Claire Hargrave, director of sales and marketing for PACCAR International, remembered the efforts of export sales director Henry Oswin, "literally camping out in Saudi Arabia for months at a time to land military and oil-field contracts." By the 1990s, thousands of Kenworth desert trucks were at work for ARAMCO in Saudi Arabia and other nations of the Middle East. What's more, nearly all of the model 853s from the original 1947 order were still in operation, rebuilt over time.

75

THE PEOPLE IN THE EXPORT DEPARTMENT at Kenworth were considered an elite group because their work was so different from domestic production. "People who viewed standard specifications as routine really enjoyed the diversity of the projects we had in export," said longtime employee and product liaison manager Larry Stanfill. PACCAR and Kenworth developed a knowledge and appreciation of the varied cultures of their international clients.

Cummins-powered W924 tankers hauled fuel through Rhodesia during the late 1960s and early 1970s along what became known as "Hell's Run."

76

In the early years, 90 percent of Kenworth exports were off-highway trucks. Many were produced at Kenworth's Canadian plant, where workers were expert at building extremely rugged trucks for that country's terrain.

WHEN RHODESIA CLOSED ITS BORDER with Zambia in the 1960s, "Hell's Run" was born. No longer could truckers deliver gasoline to Lusaka, the capital of Zambia, through Rhodesia, a 300-mile trip. Instead, the precious liquid had to be hauled 1,300 miles through the extreme terrain that gave the route its name.

Smith and Youngston, the company that had the fuel hauling contract, placed an initial order for fifty-six beefed-up Kenworth W924s with Cummins 335-horsepower engines. The rigs were custom-built to survive the 1,300-mile, five-day torture test, with a cab chassis that weighed 1,000 pounds more than that of a typical domestic model. Drivers would start at

Page 74: C500 trucks have been at work hauling hardwood logs from Indonesia's forests for a quarter century.

Previous page: Special applications for Kenworth trucks became media events, such as this 1953 rescue of a KLM Royal Dutch Airlines DC4 that had been forced down in Saudi Arabia. The Kenworth truck transported the DC4 over 4 miles of desert sand to a road and then on to the nearest repair station.

sea level from the port city of Dar es Salaam, capital of Tanzania, with a 10,000-gallon tank in tow and nothing ahead but dirt roads and an 8,000-foot mountain pass to cross before arriving five days later in Lusaka, 5,000 feet above sea level.

The sleepers on the Kenworths served another purpose: as a storage area for live chickens and sacks of rice. Food along the way was do-it-yourself. There were virtually no towns, and no coolers or truck stops.

Since the United Kingdom was subsidizing the fuel at a price of $2.80 a gallon, profit margins were high enough to pay off the trucks after just three deliveries. "But not always," recalled field service representative Dick Hogan. "Some of the drivers thought they'd make a few extra dollars on the side and would sell fuel to locals along the way." These drivers had a radical way of covering up the thefts. "They'd throw a match in the cab," Hogan said, and tell the company that the truck accidentally caught fire. "About a dozen trucks were burned, with just the frame rails and axles remaining."

Hell's Run lasted for more than six years before the border issues were resolved and more economical ways of delivering fuel were established.

KENWORTH ALSO PROSPERED when emerging nations began developing natural resources. By the early 1970s, the Southeast Asian nations of Malaysia and Indonesia represented tremendous opportunities—especially the island of Borneo, with its large forest products industry. To visit customers, a Kenworth salesman would typically fly in on a prop plane, then drive to a river to be met by a high-speed riverboat. Through swarms of mosquitoes and 100-degree temperatures with humidity to match, the boat would eventually deliver the salesman to a small river town, where a jarring drive to the customer's location awaited. "This type of travel to operation sites is the same today," Hargrave observed.

The truck used most often in the Southeast Asian jungle is the C500B, big brother of the T800—Kenworth's most popular on-road/off-road logging truck in the United States and Canada. In remote areas, grades on the muddy, rutted roads can exceed 25 percent. There are few bridges, and drivers often drive through rivers, not over them—all this with hardwood payloads that often exceed 90 tons.

While a typical North American T800 log truck has a fairly light, single-weight frame, the C500B is built to handle greater load stress. Surprisingly enough, considering the terrain, most Kenworths on Borneo are 6x4s (tandem-drive axles). With planetary hub-reduction rear axles, these

Kenworths first
went into service in
Indonesia in 1949.
Shown is a 1988
350-horsepower
model C520.

80

trucks are rated up to 100,000 pounds gross vehicle weight. The preferred engine for logging now produces between 450 and 525 horsepower with 1,450 to 1,650 foot-pounds of torque, backed up by a 15-speed or 18-speed transmission. Newer heavy-duty trucks for the Indonesian coal industry, with engines up to 600 horsepower, haul 140 tons of coal in double trailers.

Kenworths, known for their long life and for cheaper operating costs than competing European models, are considered the premium trucks for logging and mining in Southeast Asia. "We know of Kenworths that have been there nearly thirty years," said Gabriel Pepino. "They've been rebuilt, but they're still going strong."

WITH ITS REPUTATION established in the deserts of the Middle East and the jungles of Southeast Asia, Kenworth saw opportunities open around the world. Kenworth was one of thirty U.S. companies invited to the People's Republic of China in 1978 to participate in technical seminars. China, beginning to tap into its huge petroleum reserves, was impressed with Kenworth's oil-field trucks and ordered eighteen heavy-duty trucks, two small exploration vehicles, and two Super 953s similar to the model 853 rigs used in Saudi Arabia. Once oil was found, the Chinese called in U.S. companies to extract the oil and service the rigs. Those companies purchased more than 100 Kenworths.

After five years' experience with the Kenworths, the Chinese again opted for the brand, this time for use in developing the world's largest open-pit coal mine. Twelve heavy-duty C500s with lowboy trailers were used to transport some of the world's largest earthmoving equipment to the Anti Bao coal mine site in Datong, Shanxi Province.

The Chinese offered Kenworth a new problem to solve in 1993. China wanted to drill for oil in its Takla Makan Desert, home to some of the most extreme conditions Kenworth engineers ever encountered. The sand is as fine as talcum powder, and the dunes are 1,500 meters high and steeper than anything found in the Middle East—factors that make traction and stability very difficult. If that weren't enough, the desert's temperature range—from 125 degrees Fahrenheit in summer to minus 30 in winter—makes heating, cooling, and insulation foremost concerns.

Kenworth shipped a model 953 to the desert, where a contracted driver put the truck through its paces. But driver error caused an incident that ultimately helped make the deal for Kenworth. The driver misread a dune and rolled the truck. "It rolled over on a steep side-slope," recalled Bill Morse, a field representative who witnessed the mishap. "The driver was fine, just embarrassed. We righted the truck, put in fluids, and off the truck went—no worse for wear. The Chinese were very impressed, and it helped us to finalize the deal right there."

Kenworth's application of 953s for the Middle Eastern desert climate brought the company to the attention of the Chinese.

82

Although the Chinese liked the 953 in the desert, they wanted better forward visibility in order to see over the steep face of the dunes, preparing them for the downslope. They also wanted cab room for more people. Kenworth engineer John Rempel and his team came up with the solution, the Shamo Wang (Desert King)—a Super 953 with a modified cabover, instead of a conventional hood, to provide the required visibility. And it had a rear bench seat to carry six people from one oil site to another. To this day, a Kenworth is the only truck able to transport 40- to 50-ton loads through the Takla Makan Desert.

AUSTRALIA BECAME an enticing new market after a group of Australian truck operators toured the United States in 1958 to learn about equipment and transportation methods. The next year, general manager John Holmstrom traveled to Australia, liked what he saw, and managed the creation of Australian Kenworth Truck Sales Proprietary, of Doncaster, Victoria.

In 1963, Kenworth sold its first right-hand-steering truck in Australia, and the company was on the road to becoming the best-selling nameplate in that country. The move toward leadership in the market was hastened in 1966, when Australia increased tariff rates. Kenworth Australia responded by importing unassembled Kenworths to Victoria to be assembled by local labor, thus avoiding the tariffs. It soon became apparent, however, that Australia's harsh and unique operating conditions demanded trucks that were different from those required in North America. The Australian road transport industry was also just beginning a major expansion as the country's economy continued to experience significant growth, persuading Kenworth to buy land for a full manufacturing facility in Bayswater, Victoria. The 56,000-square-foot plant, with an annual production capacity of 300 trucks, was completed in late 1970. Soon after, trucks with 70 percent Australian content were coming off the line.

The most popular truck models in the 1970s and into the 1980s were bulked-up model W900s. The Australian-designed W900SAR featured a shorter bumper-to-back-of-cab measurement than the standard W900 and had a cab set higher to aid visibility and allow more cooling in the grill. Both 28-inch and 36-inch sleepers were available. The truck had a heavier frame and suspension and, as with all Australian-made Kenworths, could be equipped with a "bull bar" to deflect kangaroos and cattle roaming the outback.

Kenworth Australia designed and built many of its own models—including this cab-over-engine (COE) devised specifically for extreme Australian/New Zealand conditions.

83

Driving the outback is still considered a challenge, with terrain primitive by North American standards. Truckers haul as many as three 40-foot trailers at a time, literally becoming a rolling "road train." The legal gross combination weight limit is a huge 300,000 pounds. Even single-trailer highway applications have a higher gross cargo weight in Australia than in the U.S., by over 93,000 pounds.

"We have higher weight limits, bigger engines, and more cooling requirements, plus longer distances to travel between population centers," said Glen Walker, former chief engineer for Kenworth Australia. "That's why we have to over-engineer the trucks here. If a truck breaks down in the States, help is relatively close by. But in Australia, the driver may be many hundreds of miles away from a repair shop."

These unique operating conditions led Kenworth Australia to develop its own design and manufacturing capability. The W900SAR may have been

the first Australia-only model, but it was by no means the last. Today, all of Kenworth Australia's models are unique. Some may share nomenclature with their U.S. versions, such as the T300, but even these trucks have been designed from the ground up for Australia, Papua New Guinea, and New Zealand use.

In spite of the small size of the Australasian market, it is crowded with competitors from all over the world. Kenworth Australia's ability to design and manufacture trucks for these conditions has provided it with a major competitive advantage against other international manufacturers.

Even though tariff barriers were reduced and have now been effectively eliminated, Kenworth is the clear market leader in Australia, consistently achieving in excess of 20 percent market share.

Kenworth Australia now produces more than 1,000 units a year at a factory three times its initial size, with production split among cab-over-engine (COE) trucks, aerodynamic models, and high-hood conventionals. More than twenty dealers represent Kenworth in Australia, with dealers in New Zealand and Papua New Guinea as well. Total annual sales in 1996 exceeded $200 million.

LIKE CANADA AND AUSTRALIA, Mexico protected its economy with trade barriers. But instead of a tariff, Mexico opted for quotas on imports and for restrictions on vehicles produced in Mexico with foreign-made parts. For many manufacturers, it meant an early exit from the market. However, Kenworth saw this as an opportunity.

Already doing a healthy business through its distributor in Mexico City, Distribuidora Quintana, Kenworth knew the market. When it became clear in 1958 that sales would be cut drastically by pending import quotas, Kenworth decided to explore the possibility of building a plant in Mexico.

Kenworth sales manager Robert O'Brien held discussions with businessman Gustavo Vildosola, who was interested in converting his manufacturing plant in Mexicali to a facility that could handle the assembly of

In 1958, Mexico's Kenworth trucks were assembled outdoors with an abundance of manpower and pride.

Kenworth trucks. But the plant that manufactured trailers and storage tanks wasn't in shape to handle a conversion, or so O'Brien thought at first. "There were no walls down one side," he recalled. "It was all open toward the middle—no roof, no nothing—and a dirt floor."

So the two men worked out a trial agreement that would give Vildosola a chance to prove that his plant, with modifications, could do the job. For six months, Kenworth sent subassemblies to the plant on a consignment basis. Payment was made only after a truck was fully assembled and sold in Mexico City. Five trucks a month were produced under this agreement.

In 1960, PACCAR firmed up its relationship with the Mexicali plant by investing $100,000 for 49 percent interest in a joint venture with Vildosola and other citizens of Mexico, creating Kenworth Mexicana. Kenworth sent engineering and quality liaison Edwin Sundstrom to Mexicali to help run the operation. Many of the truck components came from the United States, but that gradually changed as local suppliers started manufacturing quality products for the plant. The facility began producing up to fifteen trucks a month in addition to trailers.

By 1976, Kenworth Mexicana was producing more than 1,100 trucks a year in a completely modern 160,000-square-foot factory in Mexicali.

Demand for the trucks eventually outstripped plant capacity, and a new facility in Mexicali on 56 acres was completed in 1970. Production increased to four trucks and two trailers per day as Kenworth became the dominant player in Mexico's trucking industry. Collapse of the peso in the late 1970s hit the country hard, and Kenworth truck production dropped to just 428 in 1977, compared with more than 1,100 the year before. More than half of Kenworth's workforce was laid off. The sale of truck parts kept the plant alive as employees waited out the economic storm.

By 1979 the economy had begun to recover. Kenworth benefited from the pent-up demand for trucks, selling nearly 2,000 that year. Some customers waited eight months for delivery, even though production was running 33 percent higher than the plant's intended capacity. Also in 1979, the plant produced its 10,000th truck.

Sales reached an all-time high of 3,023 units in 1981, mostly W900s for over-the-road use. The T800 eventually replaced the W900 and joined the aerodynamic T600 in making up nearly all of Ken-Mex's truck production. In late 1993 the Mexican economy suffered another plunge. As truck sales dwindled, PACCAR increased its ownership in Kenworth Mexicana to more than 55 percent. The currency devaluation and high interest rates

Kenworth Class 7
truck manufacturing
was transferred
from Canada to
Mexico in 1995. By
August 1995
Kenworth Mexicana
was operating at
a new record build
rate of 28 trucks
a day.

reached their peak in 1995, halting truck production at the plant for nearly six months. But PACCAR remained solidly behind the company.

PACCAR purchased the remaining shares of Ken-Mex in late 1995 and brought production of Class 7 trucks (26,000 to 33,000 pounds gross vehicle weight) to the plant. The Mexican economy started to rebound at the beginning of 1996, and a year later the plant was operating at full capacity.

THE BIG RIGS OF KENWORTH are still playing a part in development of the world's natural resources. For example, mining projects utilizing C500s are under way in Indonesia, Chile, Peru, and Russia. But the big industrial, off-road trucks that once represented 90 percent of Kenworth's export orders now account for only 10 percent; meanwhile, sales of over-the-road models have grown as road networks have expanded and transportation logistics have improved.

Kenworths are hard at work on the roads of the world, with the T800 being the truck of choice for many companies outside the United States. The K100 cabover is also popular internationally, selling more in foreign markets than in the United States due to local length regulations. Kenworths are sold in more than 40 countries. The company has succeeded globally because of its talent for customizing trucks for different uses, doing this in a way that meets the particular vehicle regulations of each country.

Opposite: Ken-Mex
Class 8 trucks are
being applied to
Mexico's growing
construction
industry.

Following pages:
The T800 line
pictured in the
1990s.

CHAPTER SIX

GOOD MOVES

The Interstate and Defense Highway Act of 1956 meant eventual construction of 42,000 miles of new or expanded roads. It would be a boon to everyone in the trucking industry, and Kenworth was ready with innovations like the tilt-cab and fiberglass hoods. In 1957 the company introduced its tilt-cab for cabover trucks, a marked improvement in ease of service. Drivers and mechanics now could simply tilt the cab forward at a 55-degree angle (later increased to as much as 90 degrees) for access to engine and transmission.

93

Two years later, that same concept took hold on a conventional truck as Unitglas construction was unveiled, with a tilt-forward hood built of fiberglass. Testing on the Alaska Highway convinced Kenworth that fiberglass had the strength to withstand the toughest conditions. Engineer Moe Buringrud said the fiberglass hood, an industry first, "solved a lot of problems that were inherent in other hood designs. Fiberglass was lighter, and it could outlast steel or aluminum hoods. Fiberglass didn't crack, tear, or rust. It twisted with the frame of the chassis, which under rough conditions could lean the cab 10 or 15 degrees in one direction, the radiator in another." The new hood, manufactured for the model 900 series, represented a weight savings of 270 pounds.

DIFFERENCES IN LAWS regulating truck sizes and weights meant that throughout the 1960s the United States was divided when it came to truck styles. The West Coast had liberalized weight, wheelbase, and length laws that allowed an overall length of 60 feet or more for a tractor-trailer combination. Conventional-design trucks with the cab behind the engine could pull trailers that were between 38 and 42 feet long. But in the Midwest and on the East Coast, overall lengths were limited to between 50 and 55 feet, depending on the state. So if you wanted to haul a 38- to 42-foot trailer, your only tractor choice was the shorter cabover design.

"For anyone wanting to go coast to coast, it was really a challenging time," recalled Al Koenig, past president of the American Truck Historical Society, owner of Midwest Specialized Transportation, and vintage Kenworth restorer and collector. "A western carrier could go as far as Denver with a conventional, then reconnect the trailer to a cabover for deliveries east of Denver. Most western states had weight limits of 70,000 pounds or more, while eastern states had limits as low as 56,000 pounds. So even if the tractor-trailer met the western limit requirements, you might have had to lighten your load before continuing east."

In the 1960s, many states recognized the problem by adopting recommended federal weight and length standards. It was the beginning of an era

that created uniformity in trucking standards, leading to the Surface Transportation Assistance Act of 1982 and to a rapid decline in use of the cabover design.

95

THE BEGINNING of the 1960s was marred by the death of Paul Pigott, whose vision of the truck manufacturing industry had guided Kenworth since its acquisition by Pacific Car and Foundry. Pigott died of a brain tumor at the age of 61. PACCAR's new leader was Robert O'Brien, who had worked as Kenworth's sales manager and later as vice president and general manager. O'Brien had joined Kenworth in 1943 and soon became Vernon Smith's chief assistant; along with a keen sense of accounting and legendary charisma, O'Brien had a talent for selling trucks. He sometimes modestly likened his role as Pacific Car's president to that of a caretaker. He served as the company's chief executive officer until Paul Pigott's son Charles was ready for the job.

From his earliest odd jobs around Pacific Car, Charles Pigott knew that he wanted to run the company. His father had seen to it that Charles began with the company's dirtiest jobs. As a teenager on summer vacations, he hauled parts, swung castings, and moved inventory around in the company's warehouse. When the Machinists' Union refused to permit him to train in Pacific Car's machine shop, he went to the company's Everett Pacific shipyard machine shop for training.

Upon college graduation, he was sent to Canadian Kenworth so that he might develop a better overview of how a division was run. He served there in a number of capacities of increasing responsibilities until 1959, when he was transferred to Seattle. Following the death of his father, Charles became an assistant vice president and then in 1962, he was made Pacific Car's executive vice president. In 1965, Charles Pigott became Pacific Car's president, and Robert O'Brien was named chairman.

FOR WESTERN BUILDERS such as Kenworth, conventional models dominated the order board in the 1960s, while cabovers were prominent for manufacturers in the eastern United States. In the early 1960s, a Kenworth was still considered a "Western truck," and more than 70 percent of orders were for conventionals. But that percentage slowly shifted toward cabovers as Kenworth established new dealerships in the Midwest and on the East Coast.

Kenworth's first dealership east of the Mississippi was Rihm Motor Company, which was founded in St. Paul, Minnesota, in 1932 and became a Kenworth dealer in 1949. "We were selling heavy equipment such as graders and shovels initially, then moved on to Hudsons and Packards, plus the Federal truck line," said Walter Rihm, whose father, John, started the company. John Rihm became interested in Kenworth after talking with Bert Roberts, of Roberts Motors in Portland, Oregon. "Bert sold him on Kenworth," Walter Rihm recalled.

"Back then, Kenworth was an unknown east of the Mississippi. People didn't even know how to pronounce the Kenworth name—they called it Kennelworth, everything but the right name. But soon enough, they'd know."

Kenworth built trucks for Rihm specifically to meet the needs of eastern companies. Rihm sold any Western truck that could be engineered for his eastern customers. Kenworths were not cheap—cabovers alone carried a $2,600 premium over eastern brands. But quality sold. "Even then, Kenworths were considered the Cadillac of the truck industry," Rihm observed. "People respected the brand."

Kenworth continued eastward expansion in the 1950s with the addition of the Kenworth Central States dealership in Chicago and two Kenworth company stores, Colorado Kenworth and Texas Kenworth. Bill Jones and Company opened a dealership in Atlanta in 1957, and Framingham Truck Sales in Framingham, Massachusetts, opened its doors soon after. Reeves

Kenworth opened in Orlando, Florida, in 1959, followed in the early 1960s by Michigan Kenworth in Detroit and HC Blackwell in Adamsville, Alabama.

To handle the growing demand for trucks in the East, Kenworth took advantage of Pacific Car and Foundry's 1958 acquisition of Dart Truck Company, using Dart's Kansas City, Missouri, factory to produce off-road vehicles, including the model 800 series of earthmovers. When the Seattle plant was hit by a lengthy strike in 1959, Dart took up the slack, and trucks continued to roll off the assembly line. Kenworth opened a $2 million

In 1955, Kenworth joined Dart Truck Company in the production of off-road trucks. Shown is a Kenworth Dart model 305-L.

97

branch factory on Dart's "back 40" in Kansas City in 1964 to accommodate more Kenworth production for eastern customers. (Following a difficult truck market in the early 1980s, PACCAR's sale of Dart, and the growing success of Kenworth's plant in Chillicothe, Ohio, the company's Kansas City plant was closed in 1986. The production slack was quickly taken up by the plants in Seattle, Chillicothe, and Ste.-Therese, Quebec.)

TWO TRUCK MODELS dominated sales at Kenworth over a period of twenty years: the W900 conventional design and the K100 cab-over-engine (COE) model. The W900 and the K100 established Kenworth as a leader in over-the-road trucks.

For many drivers, today's W900L is the majestic, long-nose conventional that defines the word truck. Its classic lines, traditional extended hood option, and chrome features celebrate the life of yesterday's and today's trucker. It's a truck for the purist. And it's the only truck still being produced with roots dating back to 1963.

The W900 series came to life when engineers designed an over-the-road model with bulkhead-style doors, cowl-mounted mirrors, a wider and taller cab, a new instrument panel, and new driver comforts. As state laws permitted longer trucks, the size of sleepers increased. A 36-inch-deep sleeper became available, followed by a 42-inch model. And in 1974 came the 60-inch VIT (Very Important Truck) flattop sleeper, the largest of its day. Drivers at last could sit on the edge of the bunk and change clothes comfortably. Two years later the company introduced a sleeper with 7 feet of head-

room—allowing a trucker to stand tall in a sleeper for the first time. The W900 sleeper of today can include a sofa that folds out to a bed, plus enough storage and other comforts to accommodate husband-and-wife teams.

One of the biggest trucking challenges ever handed to a W900 came in 1979, when the vehicle was selected to transport an immense scientific device from Illinois to California. The 107-ton unit, a high-resolution spectrometer magnet, would be used by scientists in Palo Alto, California. For the job, a custom-built W900 with a 450-horsepower CAT diesel and Spicer

24-speed compound transmission pulled an adjustable-axle trailer (with optional steering in the rear) that carried the magnet, which stood 13 feet high and measured 18 feet in diameter.

On the route to California, the truck made lots of stops to accommodate television and radio interviews. But the biggest adventure along the way before the magnet was successfully delivered came as the truck climbed over Wyoming's 8,640-foot Laramie Summit in 60-mile-per-hour winds. Driver Stan Jones remembered it well: "You're squinting into a blizzard, shifting with both hands, steering with both knees, pulling a 110-wheel trailer with more angles and dangles than the Golden Gate Bridge. Then you begin to feel ice on the road. That's when you thank the man upstairs that you're driving a Kenworth."

In 1982, Kenworth engineers designed the W900B. The marine plywood floor of the original W900 was replaced by lighter aluminum. A new roof cap smoothed air flow, and the ride was improved thanks to a new taper-leaf spring design. The rig would evolve from there and continue to draw the smiles of truck aficionados like Al Koenig. "Appearance-wise, I think the latest W900 is the greatest thing Kenworth has ever done. The W900L presents an image that represents the very soul of trucking."

SHORTLY AFTER THE W900 debuted in 1963, Kenworth engineers shifted their attention to cabovers, and the K100 was launched. With its tilt-cab design, the K100 was unlike other cabovers on the market. It was available in aluminum and in four different bumper-to-back-of-cab sizes: 52, 73,

102

In 1979, a 450-horsepower, CAT-diesel W900, hauling a huge scientific device known as a high-resolution spectrometer magnet, climbs toward Wyoming's Laramie Summit in a snowy 60-mile-an-hour wind.

76, and 86 inches, with the last three including sleeper compartments. What's more, the new Kenworth offered more horsepower and transmission options than trucks made by the company's eastern competitors.

The K100s slowly gained in popularity with the start of production at the Kenworth plant in Kansas City and with continued expansion of dealerships, such as Hissong-Kenworth, and Truck Enterprises in Harrisonburg, Virginia, plus new company dealerships in Kansas City and in Omaha, Nebraska. The new Kansas City plant "demonstrated our resolve to grow nationwide," said Bill Gross, Kenworth's first eastern region sales manager and later general manager of Kenworth. "At the start, Kenworths were a hard sell. Customers were skeptical. Kenworths were different. But after customers began using the truck, they saw the quality."

1963 marked the beginning of the modern Kenworth era with the introduction of the W900 (at left) and the K100.

The K100 series also evolved. As laws permitted longer trucks, new sleeper sizes and options were introduced. Cosmetically, trucks followed automobile trends as headlights changed from round to rectangular. The exterior was smoothed to cut wind resistance, a new suspension system gave a softer ride, and set-back axle options increased maneuverability. In 1984 a redesigned cab and interior gave drivers an even better working environment.

Today, with laws on vehicle length no longer giving truckers an incentive to use short tractors, cabovers represent a small percentage of the industry's total sales of Class 8 trucks. Yet they still have a following. Among K100 drivers, perhaps none is more ardent than Henry Good.

As long as he can remember, Good has been fascinated by the big rigs. "I wanted to drive since I was a little boy," he recalled. "My mom tried to talk me out of it. She even gave me flying lessons, but that didn't help." He drove a farm truck when he was twelve, moved to delivery trucks in high school, and on his twenty-first birthday took his road test and got a commercial license. He bought his first truck, a 1974 Kenworth cabover, in 1976, and five years later purchased a new K100 Aerodyne: "This was the truck I'd been waiting for." Several months later, Good found a name for his new Kenworth. He was traveling the interstate, chatting with a couple over his CB radio. They asked what amenities he had inside his truck, and Good reported "a refrigerator, two TVs, closets, you name it."

106

"Dang, Hank," came the reply, "you've got a Highway Hilton."

Good's truck, after more than 1.5 million miles, still features the original paint job—with "Highway Hilton" now inscribed on it. More than 150 running lights, along with the lighted initials "HG" in the center of the grill, make the truck a can't-miss attraction. Lots of chrome rounds out the styling. "Ninety percent of truckers think it looks great," Good said. "Ten percent think it's a bit much. But I like it and I'll never sell it."

A HEALTHY TRUCKING INDUSTRY meant more sales for Kenworth, as the number of its domestic dealerships increased to forty-six in 1966. The nation's freight tonnage was ever-increasing, and with it came the need for more trucks. Thanks to new highways, the time for a typical run from the Midwest to the West Coast was cut by as much as a day; for a run across the entire country, by up to two days. Just over 35,000 Class 8 trucks were registered in the United States in 1962; ten years later the number exceeded 120,000. It was a decade of prosperity for truck builders—especially Kenworth, as it saw its market share double during the same time period, topping 7.6 percent in 1972.

The W900 and K100 led the way in sales, with innovations that made the models even more attractive. For instance, Kenworth's proprietary twin-axle torsion-bar suspensions were lighter and offered a more comfortable ride than the suspension systems offered by other truck manufacturers. A new method of ordering trucks helped the company keep up with customer demand, which reached more than 2,000 trucks in 1964, then jumped to 3,000 in 1965. Kenworth's "order selection criteria" system provided a

Completed K100 cabs await their mounting to chassis on a Kenworth final assembly line.

In 1976 Kenworth introduced the industry's first raised-roof sleeper, the Aerodyne. Initial production was a special version called the VIT 200 Bicentennial Edition, to coincide with America's 200th birthday.

computerized method of cross-checking truck specifications for compatibility. This helped free precious engineering time, allowing Kenworth to maintain its tradition of custom truck building. Truck production kept increasing, with a 1971 total of more than 6,600, creating the need for a new plant, which was built in Chillicothe, Ohio, and opened in 1974.

The Surface Transportation Assistance Act of 1982, which ended the practice of counting a tractor's length when determining whether a trucking rig meets length restrictions, brought a big decline in production of the K100 cabover. Its last big year was 1984, when the company produced more than 7,000 of the trucks. Two years later, the total dropped to fewer than 2,000. In comparison, 6,000 Kenworth conventional truck models were produced in 1984, increasing to nearly 9,000 in 1986.

Kenworth dealers had a potent ally in their sales efforts in the form of PACCAR financing. Beginning in 1970, PACCAR Financial Corporation (PFC) gave potential customers a way to buy a Kenworth without having to arrange financing through a bank that might or might not understand trucking. When interest rates soared in 1981, PFC offered financing as low as 3 percent below market rates. PFC also became the first in the industry to offer customers the option to refinance at lower rates, should market rates fall.

PACCAR Leasing Corporation was formed in 1980 to provide the legal, financial, and marketing framework for dealers interested in entering the field of full-service truck rental and leasing. PacLease created a franchise-based system that meant more truck sales for Kenworth and new growth opportunities for its dealers.

BUSINESS WAS ALSO GOOD in Canada. Whereas freight movement in the United States was shifting from trains to trucks, railroads were still the principal transporters in Canada. But natural-resources industries provided ample opportunity for early Kenworth factory branches and dealers, such as Inland Kenworth, which began operation in Penticton, British Columbia, in 1957. With Kenworth's Burnaby plant and its engineering staff dedicated to Canadian trucks, it didn't take long for Kenworth to command a market share of 30 percent or more.

"It helped tremendously to have the Burnaby factory," recalled Leigh Parker, whose father, Lloyd, founded Inland Kenworth. "Trucks were built specifically for our applications and conditions. Most of our business was in logging, and the guys would work the woods mostly in the winter. You needed a special breed of truck to handle 20-below temperatures and roads of ice."

A Canadian cab-over-engine (COE) model.

Farther east, Mike King was helping Kenworth gain a foothold in Edmonton, Alberta. In 1957, the oil industry played an important part in Kenworth sales, as it does to this day. "A big truck here was an LW924 with a 220 Cummins and 44,000-pound double-reduction rear ends," observed King, who went on to buy Kenworth's Edmonton branch in 1982. "It [LW924] wasn't a sexy truck, but it had a reputation of strength."

Slowly, general freight began playing a role for Canadian Kenworth dealers as highway systems developed. In Edmonton, cabovers began selling to truckers who carried beef to the East Coast and returned with general freight. By 1974, over-the-road trucks made up more than 60 percent of Edmonton's business.

Pacific Car and Foundry's Sicard plant in Ste.-Therese, Quebec, began building K100 cabovers for eastern Canadian and U.S. markets, and the plant later became a Canadian Kenworth facility. During this period a new model was introduced and was produced at the Ste.-Therese facility: the low cab forward Hustler. This refuse pickup vehicle evolved into the L700 and featured dual steering, permitting operators to drive from either the left or right side, using a gear shift in the middle. Kenworth sold its last L700 in 1987, but the design lived on under the Peterbilt moniker, which shared the same engineering.

In its infancy, Canadian Kenworth had manufactured 60 to 100 trucks a year in its small Burnaby plant. Canadian Kenworth's accomplishments included the model 849RFD, the largest logging truck ever produced—a behemoth that could haul loads up to a half-million pounds.

Canadian Kenworth expanded its off-road truck manufacturing capabilities when it began assembling trucks at the Sicard plant in Ste.-Therese. Pacific Car had acquired Sicard in 1967 and later moved Kenworth truck manufacturing to Ste.-Therese. By then Canadian Kenworth matched the U.S. sales growth rate in heavy-duty trucks and specialized vehicles. In 1982 the Burnaby plant was closed; from then on the western Canadian market was supplied from the Seattle plant.

Beginning in the 1960s, custom-engineered C500s were manufactured for service in North America's frigid Arctic oil fields.

AS KENWORTH PROGRESSED in over-the-road truck engineering, manufacturing, and sales, it never gave up its roots in off-highway models. Because early roads in the West were few and rough, early Kenworths were built as much for off-road as for highway use.

Company management knew the value of off-highway truck engineering to Kenworth's over-the-road models. "We'd take on a lot of special-purpose projects not only to satisfy a customer need, but to test Kenworth systems in real, and often hostile, environments," recalled Bill Gross. "Kenworth learned a great deal about insulation from trucks designed for the Arctic, and much about heating and cooling systems from trucks for the desert."

While trucks destined for the oil fields of the Middle East were often the most complex, the remote and rugged environment of Canada also offered plenty of challenge. In the mid 1960s, models with gross vehicle weights of up to 180,000 pounds were developed for far-northern customers. The model 850, which came later, was so robust that loggers could pull two and sometimes three trailers, each with 100 tons of logs, from the woods to the mill. Kenworth also developed trucks for coal haulers in Canada and West Virginia.

As virgin old-growth timber gave way to second-generation trees in the 1970s, the W900 became the truck of choice. "That truck became a legend unto itself," observed John Rempel, engineering manager for off-highway and specialty trucks. "We took the W900 design further—making it stouter by beefing up the front suspension and cab mounting area."

The heavy logger known as LW924 was hard to miss. A sheet-metal hood and fender arrangement made it better suited to off-road conditions, and the "hard-boiled radiator," as it was called, featured an over-size steel-top tank that became a structural feature of the truck. "It stood out nice and proud in the weather," noted Rempel. "That radiator didn't fail, and that meant the difference between getting to the destination and breaking down on the road."

The oil fields of Canada posed other problems. An oil field rarely finds its place near a highway, so you have to go over virgin territory to get there. In northern conditions, with high frost in spring and fall, the terrain is soft—and it's not unusual for trucks to operate in mud that's 2 or 3 feet deep. Kenworth became the favored truck for Canadian oil fields, and it remains so today, especially the C550B with tandem steering.

Today Kenworth builds specialized trucks at the rate of 250 to 400 per year—vehicles that, as Rempel put it, "withstand the rigors of the absolute worst conditions you can throw at a truck." In designing a specialized truck, he said, "We don't often start with a clean piece of paper. We're always adapting and developing a better truck for tomorrow based on the experiences gained today."

At work in the woods of northern Maine, this C520 was designed for heavy-duty, off-road hauls.

CHAPTER SEVEN

MORE THAN A NEW LOOK

Operating costs were looming ever larger in the minds of Kenworth's customers in the late 1970s and early 1980s, and the company weighed possible design improvement. The result was the T600, with aerodynamic design that gave a huge boost to fuel efficiency.

The story of the T600 begins with the Arab embargo on oil sales to the United States in late 1973 and early 1974 and the subsequent rapid increase in fuel costs. Engineer Larry Orr had a lot of time to daydream while he waited to fill the gas tank in his car. "Sitting in those legendary lines for gas is what got me thinking about fuel economy," he recalled. "I knew we could improve fuel economy on heavy trucks by improving their aerodynamics."

In 1976, as director of research and development for PACCAR, Orr began doing some homework in aerodynamics. He shared his vision with Tim Kangas, assistant director of research and development, who had extensive experience in wind tunnel testing. The two men created wood and wax models, testing different shapes and configurations, most often at the University of Washington's wind tunnel.

Midway through the research, Orr was promoted to Kenworth as its chief engineer. "During the early 1980s," Orr remembered, "the market had begun to fall sharply, and the country was in a serious recession by 1982. The project was off more than it was on." But Orr's group finally was able to build a prototype and run tests on the aerodynamic truck at the PACCAR Technical Center. "It proved out the whole idea of aerodynamics and fuel economy," he recalled.

115

The experimental-
concept "KX."

Page 114: Since its
release in 1985, the
T600A has evolved,
into the T600B
Aerodyne sleeper
(shown) and finally
to the T600 AeroCab.

Previous page:
Recognizing that a
significant portion
of the fuel con-
sumed by a truck is
due to air resis-
tance, Kenworth
began applying
aerodynamic princi-
ples to truck design
in 1977. Shown is
the concept "KX"
cabover (right),
which eventually
gave way to the
design of the T600
(left).

THERE WAS ONLY ONE PROBLEM: Orr and his team had developed an aerodynamic cabover model. The new truck was conceived during the time that cab-over-engine (COE) designs were in demand: in the early 1980s, more than half of the long-haul trucks on the road were cabovers. But trucking laws no longer gave an advantage to short tractors, and the conventional long-nose trucks again dominated the Class 8 market. Orr noted that by the time he and his team had figured out the new aerodynamic cabover, "the rules had changed and conventionals were the future. We had to go back to the drawing board."

THE KENWORTH TEAM took the conventional model W900B as its benchmark in creating aerodynamic design applications. Wind tunnel tests on molded clay models gave favorable results. "Getting management's approval to take the radical truck design to the next level was a whole other matter," Orr mused, "but we got approval to go further." After more than a year of testing and revision, the team's aerodynamic conventional was ready for prototype development. It had a sloped hood, lowered bumpers, sleek fenders, side skirts, roof fairings, and an air cleaner placed under the hood. The T600 looked far different from anything on the road.

Truck drivers are always willing to consider technological changes, but they like the looks of conventional trucks. Orr was aware that the new design would likely meet some resistance, so he started out conservatively. "We had other ideas which would have made the T600 even more radical-looking. But we didn't want to introduce too much too soon."

While the T600's most prominent feature, the sloped hood, drew most of the attention, the truck was loaded with other innovations. A set-back front axle allowed for easier front axle loading. New 64-inch taper-leaf springs provided a much improved ride, and the turning radius was 23 percent less than on other conventional trucks. The new design reduced splash and spray by 50 percent, to the great benefit of other vehicles on the road.

But the truck's biggest selling point was economy. "The fuel economy numbers we got in wind tunnel testing were pretty significant," Orr said, "and we were confident that those numbers would prove themselves out—but we had to do some real-life testing to confirm our calculations."

The first step was taking a standard W900B and computing its fuel use at the PACCAR test track. Then the hood was removed and the truck was reconfigured like the T600, while leaving the power train and other components as is. Around the track the new hybrid went, slipping its way through the wind with 22 percent more fuel efficiency than the W900B.

119

ORR CREATED QUITE A STIR when he first drove the truck to Kenworth headquarters. The comments started immediately. "Half said it was the most unusual truck they ever saw; some just shook their heads," Orr recalled. "It wasn't the warmest reception." But Kenworth management was willing to give the T600 a try. Kenworth knew it had a potential winner from a fuel economy standpoint, as well as improvements in maneuverability, visibility, and ride.

The first production model T600 rolled off the Seattle assembly line in the spring of 1985.

Real-world testing came next. Two T600s made their way from Phoenix, Arizona, to Miami Beach, Florida. One was equipped with a Cummins Formula L10 270-horsepower engine, the other with a Formula 350 Big Cam IV rated at 350 horsepower. The results were clearly significant. The lower-powered T600 averaged 9 miles per gallon, while the T600 with the Big Cam achieved nearly 8 miles per gallon. The next step was convincing dealers and customers.

The truck was officially introduced at Kenworth's 1985 dealer meeting. "My reaction to the T600 was very positive," said Hatch Barrett, president of Trebar Kenworth Sales in Boise, Idaho. "I took to it right away and was probably more complimentary about its looks than a lot of people. The aerodynamic advantages were so obvious that anyone who didn't jump on that bandwagon would be out of the band."

"Radical, European, and no chrome—that's what I remember thinking," recalled Ken Hoffman, executive vice president of Ozark Kenworth in Kansas City. "It was such a radical change that I think other manufacturers would have had a tough time with it; Kenworth's reputation opened the doors. We own a number of stores, and the salespeople who really believed in the concept and what it had to offer really had great years. There's no doubt the T600 revolutionized the industry."

Previous pages: Kenworth dealers were introduced to the T600 in 1985. By the end of that year, the new model represented almost 40 percent of Kenworth's new business.

The truck's fuel economy numbers were too substantial to ignore: the first users of the T600 saw a significant reduction in fuel bills, which accounted for 20 to 25 percent of operating costs. By year's end, T600 sales represented more than 40 percent of Kenworth's new business. "We could barely keep up with demand," Orr said with a grin. "I knew there would be a lot of owner-operators and fleets who would be hesitant to buy the truck because of its shape. But I also knew there were good businesspeople out there who would recognize its potential."

FOR MANY FLEET BUYERS, there is an attitude of "you first" when new technology comes along. With the industry so price-competitive, companies can't afford to make a mistake on capital equipment. Many buyers backed off when they saw the T600. But Glenn Brown, president of Joplin, Missouri-based Contract Freighters, Inc. (CFI), stepped forward.

In 1995, the original T600A development team was presented with the National Award for the Advancement of Motor Vehicle Research and Development. From left: Rich Drollinger, Larry Orr, Roy Meriman, Don Richardson, and Wayne Simons.

CFI had nearly 500 leased operators working for the company, but wanted to bring on its own trucks. Brown looked closely at the T600. "I recognized that it was innovative and different. We were looking for ways to improve our efficiencies and decided to order 100 of the trucks. We were hoping that the new design of the T600 was something we could use to get a head start on the rest of the industry. It was definitely a gamble to be the first in the market to put the truck on the road, but it proved out."

The T600 offered more than good looks and fuel efficiency. It also offered a better ride and shorter turning radius.

124

Although the new Kenworth improved on CFI's fleet average for fuel efficiency by about 1.5 miles per gallon, Brown's drivers were not quick to accept the truck. "It took them about a year to adapt to the looks of the T600," he said. "It's hard to believe, but I had some drivers come into my office literally in tears, threatening to quit if I made them drive what they called the 'anteater.' They were ribbed in truck stops and on the CB." But that changed as drivers became accustomed to the truck's new look and to its record-setting efficiency. Today, CFI runs more than 1,800 T600s in its fleet.

While the principal testament to the T600's success has been the number of orders for the truck since its introduction in 1985—more than 80,000 were on the road by 1997—the Kenworth engineering team on the project also received the U.S. Department of Transportation's National Award for the Advancement of Motor Vehicle Research and Development, in recognition of the T600's advancements in safety, energy savings, and reduced environmental impact.

THE AERODYNAMIC DESIGN of the T600 also came to life in another new truck designed for tough use both off and on the highway. This new model, the T800, began giving competition in 1986 to the W900, long regarded as Kenworth's do-all truck. Sporting a sloped hood, set-back axle design, and chrome and polish options, the T800 quickly became a top seller in the construction and logging industries. Kenworth upped the ante in the heavy-haul marketplace in 1993 when it introduced the T800 Heavy Hauler, with a larger radiator and grill to handle up to 550-horsepower engines in extreme applications.

The T800 served as the workhorse for an unusual operation in 1991, when Kenworth teamed with longtime customer Schmitt Lowbed Services, of Redding, California, to move a rare SR-71 Blackbird spy plane from the Mojave Desert to Seattle's Museum of Flight.

Five Kenworth trucks were used in moving the 98-foot plane. A T800 with a Caterpillar 460-horsepower engine and a specially made 73-foot Trail King trailer transported the fuselage. Four other Kenworths handled the engines and wing sections. After twelve days of careful travel, mostly on back roads during nighttime hours, the Kenworths and the Blackbird arrived safely at the Museum of Flight, where the plane is now a star attraction.

125

In 1991, five Kenworths transported a retired SR-71 Blackbird spy plane from the Mojave Desert to the Museum of Flight in Seattle, with a T800 carrying the 98-foot plane.

Kenworth reengineered its line of Class 7 trucks to include conventional models such as the T300 shown here.

Previous pages: Full-size T800 with giant earthmoving equipment.

THE SMALL-TRUCK MARKET has always been challenging. During the 1920s, Vernon Smith made a deal for delivery of unassembled small Diamond T trucks that were sold as the Kenworth model VS, because Kenworth could not produce its own small trucks at a profit. During the 1930s, Kenworth sold Studebaker's light trucks. But after the Depression, Kenworth concentrated on the heavy-duty truck market.

In 1986, PACCAR contracted with Volkswagen for Brazilian-made delivery trucks that became the Kenworth model 300 Mid-Ranger. The Mid-Ranger, a basic cabover truck, afforded Kenworth an economical way to enter the Class 7 market without costly investments in design and manufacturing facilities. The model 300 offered a Cummins engine, Rockwell axles, and Fuller transmissions as standard equipment. Its design was modified in 1992, and production was moved from Brazil to Kenworth's Ste.-Therese plant.

In 1994, based on Kenworth's experience with the Mid-Ranger, the company developed the T300, its first conventional-design truck for the Class 7 market. Its design was based on the engineering and aerodynamics of the T600.

The T300 featured a modified T600 cab, a gross vehicle weight of up to 33,000 pounds, and a tractor rated at 65,000 pounds (gross combination weight rating). The T300 chassis—which became everything from dump truck to delivery truck—was produced at Ste.-Therese.

Prior to the T300, Kenworth's share of Class 7 truck sales had been steady but small. This was in part due to Kenworth's overall manufacturing capacity: well beyond the first half of the 1990s, all Kenworth plants were at full capacity producing Class 8 models. In 1996, T300 production was moved to Mexicali, where total truck volume soon reached the plant's full capacity of 28 trucks per day.

CHAPTER EIGHT

READY FOR THE FUTURE

The Kenworth story throughout the 1980s and into the 1990s is a tale of evolutionary change spurred by competition and the demands of a changing economy. By the close of the 1970s, Kenworth was essentially a two-product company, with the K100 cabover and enduring W900 representing the biggest volume of over-the-road truck sales. Over the next decade, market share climbed as the product line expanded. Kenworth continued to build on its tradition of innovation, making new corporate commitments to quality and to research and development as it kept competitive in a world market.

131

The years following the oil crisis of 1973 were kind to the domestic truck industry. By the late 1970s, the prolonged boom had reached the point that the Kenworth plants in Chillicothe, Ste.-Therese, and Kansas City couldn't keep pace with the backlog of orders for the K100 and the W900. At the Seattle plant, a retooling of the assembly line increased W900 capacity to thirty-four trucks a day. "Demand seemed to increase with our capacity to build trucks," recalled Seattle production veteran Dan Cleveland. "We worked long hours plus a lot of weekends just to keep pace with customer demand."

In an industry noted for its cycles of boom and bust, however, several truck makers found themselves ill-prepared for the economic downturn of 1982, when domestic registration of Class 8 trucks fell to about half the 1979 level. With the bottom falling out of the market, some manufacturers sought reorganization under bankruptcy laws. Overseas competitors were quick to take advantage, and a number of weakened U.S. truck makers were consolidated into European corporations.

WHILE HARD HIT BY THE POOR ECONOMY, Kenworth fared better than most, thanks to strong vocational market niches and customer loyalty, plus the financial strength of PACCAR. Nevertheless, production in 1982 amounted to only 7,207 trucks—less than half the 1979 total. Order backlogs dried up, and Kenworth plants were forced to cut work hours and lay off workers. "Things changed quickly," confirmed Cleveland, then a general foreman. "There's nothing better than being too busy in the truck manufacturing business, but there's nothing worse than having to let good people go."

Gary Moore, PACCAR vice president of quality, purchasing, and logistics, agreed that it was a tough time to be in the trucking industry, and fears of overseas competition were growing. Kenworth was concerned that the Asian manufacturers would take the opportunity to enter into the North American Class 8 market and that the offshore manufacturers could potentially come to dominate the industry as they had the domestic automotive business. Moore said, "We were putting a quality, cost-effective product on the road, but we didn't want to find ourselves in the position of the Big Three, trying to compete against a cookie cutter product."

Throughout PACCAR and Kenworth, there was a sense of urgency. Observed Moore: "I think that's what really spearheaded our move toward formalizing quality processes throughout the company."

132

THE DECADE AFTER THE 1982 RECESSION saw the culture of Kenworth evolve into one of collaboration between management and employees to improve products, and the company became even more market-driven. When Gary Moore became Seattle plant manager in 1981, he said, "there was a deeply ingrained, old-fashioned management style," a near-adversarial relationship with employees. So Moore helped develop a system called Quality of Worklife, built on programs that were successful at the Kenworth plant in Kansas City. The idea was to involve employees in all aspects of the business.

Quality of Worklife brought better communications, understanding, and an open exchange of ideas, helping focus Kenworth's efforts on quality, safety, and productivity. "We took a plant like Seattle that was always successful, and from a human relations standpoint, the program moved us forward to the next level," Moore said, "better production and better trucks."

According to Marilyn Santangelo, a former director of quality for Kenworth, the new direction changed the company forever. "We had never given production employees credit for their understanding of the production process," she said. "Before Quality of Worklife, a small number of people in management were looked to for answers to problems. Of course, there's no way they could have a complete picture of the situation."

133

With Quality of Worklife established at all plants, PACCAR conducted its own quality audit of Kenworth in 1983. The results were good, but they indicated the truck maker could do more. Kenworth developed an even more aggressive program, the Kenworth Quality Audit, with firmer measurements of quality and establishment of uniform practices among all plants.

Kenworth proposed a quality management program to PACCAR that was put to work in all divisions in 1986 as the PACCAR Integrated Quality System. Every function—from engineering, materials, and manufacturing to sales and customer service—was measured as part of quality assessment. The program helped direct Kenworth toward the objectives of high quality, high value, and defect-free products, along with service that exceeds customer expectations.

The program also set the stage for Kenworth's certification by the International Standards Organization, the Geneva-based body composed of national standards agencies from ninety-one nations. The ISO 9001 standard designates the mark of the highest level of systems for quality assurance in design, development, manufacturing, and testing. Kenworth was the first U.S. heavy-duty truck manufacturer to attain the ISO 9001 concurrent certification for all of its domestic truck manufacturing facilities.

MANY OF THE CHANGES at Kenworth in the 1980s and 1990s had their roots in 1977, when PACCAR chairman Charles Pigott assigned Don Stephens the task of developing a technical center. "It was an expression of Mr. Pigott's long view of the business and Kenworth's future position in the trucking industry," the retired PACCAR engineer recalled two decades later.

Stephens visited more than two dozen technical centers across the country, learning what worked and what didn't. His mission was to design and build the trucking industry's premier testing facility. Pigott and Stephens selected a location in Skagit County, Washington, and construction of the PACCAR Technical Center was completed in 1982.

The new facility, on 243 wooded acres near Padilla Bay, was built to test new components and developments in truck design. Findings are now used to improve truck quality, safety, and fuel economy, as well as to reduce

135

The PACCAR Technical Center was completed in 1982 on a 243-acre site near Mount Vernon, Washington.

noise and other emissions from on-highway vehicles. The Technical Center is well funded and features the latest equipment for testing and product evaluation. These include an environmental dynamometer, a ride simulator, a failure analysis laboratory, and high-speed computers for analyzing the durability of truck parts. An extensive proving ground offers both a level durability route and a 1.4-mile banked, high-speed oval track. Even the approach to truck testing is changing. Today, the Center cooperates with Kenworth during design, both analyzing and testing components, so that the test of the completed truck will be only a confirmation of a successful design.

ABOUT THE TIME the Technical Center was completed, Kenworth's Research and Development Lab found a permanent home in Renton, Washington. The small group of development engineers had been housed in various locations since the lab was first established in the early 1970s.

With the resources of the Technical Center available, the development lab could focus its energies on product development rather than the testing of existing components. It was this freedom of engineering creativity, according to Gary Moore, that established Kenworth as the industry's leader in innovation.

Development of the aerodynamic T600 fuel-efficient truck has been the most significant accomplishment in a long line of development lab innovations. "It was a difficult time," recalled Wayne Simons, research and development manager. "We were just emerging from the recession of the early 1980s, and budgets were tight. However, management let us continue research and development."

The T600 established a new standard for the industry, one that forever positioned Kenworth as the industry's technology leader and innovator. Subsequent development lab efforts have included aerodynamic mirrors, the T800, the AeroCab integrated sleeper, and the prototype for Kenworth's truck for the new century, the T2000. The PACCAR Technical Center was a partner in bringing these product advancements to reality.

Since the Depression, PACCAR has always recorded a profit for stockholders. A primary reason for this success has been the company's willingness to invest in research and development. "Because of this commitment," said David Hovind, PACCAR president and former Kenworth manager, "we have always seemed to be able to catch the industry off guard and surprise our competition with new product introductions and with innovative changes to existing models."

The Technical Center's durability course measures the effect of rough roads on Kenworth trucks.

Opposite: A T600
VIT model AeroCab,
utilizing aluminum
and fiberglass
construction, was
introduced in 1993.

THE BIRTH OF THE T600 AeroCab illustrates Kenworth's new technological capabilities. The AeroCab challenge to engineering was daunting: design an integrated, modular-construction cab/sleeper with a potpourri of driver amenities, while maintaining Kenworth's tradition of durability—and have it ready for production within a year.

Initial market review, product definition, and design work began in September 1992. Ten short months later, the AeroCab, one of Kenworth's most innovative products ever, was introduced at the International Trucking Show in Anaheim, California. It marked the swiftest new-product development in company history.

Work on the AeroCab began with input from all facets of the company. Initial schematics and computer design were followed by construction of a mock-up. Within months, the first true prototype was completed at the Development Lab. Prototype testing at the Technical Center led to computer three-dimensional stress analysis, allowing engineers to fine-tune areas of concern.

"This technology helped us determine how different materials affect structural strength," explained Paul Middelhoven, Kenworth's chief engineer at the time. "It allowed us to strengthen some areas, and in other areas of low stress, it allowed us to use lighter materials. The end result is a stronger and lighter truck." And, he added, "it set the stage for future product developments such as the T2000."

This 1923 laminated, leather-topped, windowless Kenworth cab illustrates how far cab design has come.

CHAPTER NINE

THE MAKING OF THE T2000

The 1990s brought forth a radically new truck for Kenworth, a cutting edge design that would set the standard of Kenworth for the new millennium. The T2000 represented the use of new technology and materials to turn the ideas of driving professionals into reality, backed by 60,000 hours of testing. The T2000 would become the best demonstration of what Kenworth had learned during three-quarters of a century of designing and building trucks.

141

The eight-member team that met for the first time in May 1992 was given a challenging list of objectives for the new truck: reduce drag and increase fuel efficiency; use new composite materials for a lighter, stronger truck with increased payload; improve cab visibility and livability—and deliver the new truck within three years. Kenworth's senior managers had also decided they wanted the T2000 to look "appreciably different than anything on the road."

The team of engineers and managers representing design, manufacturing, parts, and marketing went to work. Engineers drew on expertise they had gained in designing the integrated sleeper cab that became the AeroCab. That project began with suggestions from the Kenworth Drivers' Board, a group of more than 500 professional drivers. The drivers gave engineers new ideas, and also verified what many engineers experienced after spending time on the road with full-time truckers. The Drivers' Board suggestions included a wider opening to the sleeper compartment, more storage space, longer closets, and a seat that would better accommodate both long- and short-legged drivers.

Page 140: The T2000 was designed to be both distinctive and efficient. It was introduced to the industry in mid-1996.

Previous page: Early concepts of the T2000 underwent extensive wind tunnel testing.

THE AEROCAB, mounted on a T600 chassis, was introduced in July 1993, and within a year it represented more than 50 percent of orders for the T600. The same development process was later applied to designing an advanced model called the Studio Sleeper. Kenworth engineers now drew on observations of the Drivers' Board to begin the three-year, $100 million process of creating the T2000.

One engineering group worked with computer software and three-dimensional modeling technology that could produce anything from a wax model of a fender to an entire truck scaled to one-tenth of actual size. The scale models were used to prove new concepts in aerodynamics. With computer technology and dimensional modeling, engineers could now move from theory to testing in a matter of hours instead of weeks. With each design change—an increased angle for the windshield, a finer taper for the hood— new models were subjected to hours of wind tunnel testing. Fine-tuning the design sometimes returned to engineering intuition, and offending surfaces were hand-sanded to achieve optimum air flow.

A prototype of the interior of the proposed T2000 cab toured the country and was shown at truck stops. More than 1,200 drivers had a chance to inspect it and make suggestions for improvements. The new truck needed a

142

The evolution of the T600: original T600A (left), T600B with modular Aerodyne sleeper (center), and T600 AeroCab.

radiator configured to allow for increased cooling capacity while accommodating the low profile necessary for good aerodynamics. The development team came up with what engineering coordinator Wayne Simons termed a cross-flow radiator—a departure from traditional designs, which were vertical. The ergonomics engineers at the PACCAR Technical Center advised on such things as the angle of the steering wheel in relation to the truck's instrumentation. When they were done, the truck's controls looked more like the cockpit of a fighter plane than the cab of a ground-bound freight hauler.

Engineers had already developed the aerodynamic properties of the T600 as far as technology would allow, so entirely new design criteria were developed for the T2000. Aerodynamically, it would be new from the ground up. "On our early designs, we didn't pay much attention to styling," Simons observed. "We just tried to get the drag coefficient as low as possible." As the aerodynamics were being refined, "we'd go back and forth until we reached a shape that was in the right direction and still aesthetically pleasing. Aerodynamics was important, but so was styling. The T2000 had to have the right combination."

New materials, such as boron fiber structural members for the cab, meant new manufacturing methods, including use of robots at Kenworth's Chillicothe plant. Testing of the new materials proved their durability: steel would break before the bonded fiber structure would delaminate. The fiber technology was patterned after similar materials used in building the Boeing 777.

The first T2000 prototype, referred to by the development group as the "Green Truck," was completed in December 1993, only eighteen months after the project began. By this time the development team—which included T600 veteran engineer Larry Orr, Kenworth chief engineer Paul Middelhoven, manager Jim Bechtold of the PACCAR Technical Center, and project manager Rob Chopp—had grown to more than seventy members. The full-scale prototype was powered by a 550-horsepower Cummins engine, and the cab included the best of the elements proven in wind tunnel testing. And much to the pleasure of company management, the look was dramatically different from anything else on the road.

THE NEW TRUCK had about 30 percent fewer component parts than the T600, but they were more complex. Kenworth's heady objectives for the truck's durability—an optional 350,000-mile warranty, reduced maintenance time, a life expectancy of 2 million miles—significantly raised the bar for performance from parts suppliers.

PACCAR chairman Charles Pigott repeated again and again: "The foundation for the company's success—both past and future—evolves from the integrity of the quality of our products." It was this mantra that enabled Kenworth to increase the life expectancy of its trucks from 1 to 2 million miles in the period of a decade.

Kenworth recognized that modern competitive trucking required high-tech solutions. And its suppliers developed innovative new parts for the T2000. Eaton came up with a wheel seal with a life expectancy of 350,000 miles, about double that of the seals used on other trucks, and Spicer created a drive line that decreased the need for lubrication by a factor of almost 7 (from every 15,000 miles to once every 100,000 miles).

145

The Technical Center was key to the development of the T2000, testing the prototype to its points of failure. PACCAR's Purchasing and Corporate Quality divisions were involved as well. In the early 1980s, truck parts were being acquired from more than 1,200 suppliers, and more than 50 percent of the company's warranty work was the result of supplied parts. By 1995 the number of suppliers had been reduced by more than half. The Purchasing and Corporate Quality divisions began inspecting the suppliers' facilities, auditing their quality programs, and choosing the best, which were designated as Preferred Suppliers.

Before the T2000 was approved for release, it completed the equivalent of 5 million miles of durability evaluation. Testing went beyond the Technical Center tracks. Cooling-system test runs over Washington state's Stevens Pass offered steep ascents and descents, from near sea level to more than 4,000 feet. The T2000 also went to Minnesota for subzero evaluation of its climate control system. As testing neared an end, Kenworth began the year-long job of building the specialized tooling and assembly systems needed by the Chillicothe plant, which would manufacture the new trucks.

THE T2000 WAS NEW, inside and out. Its hood and cab doors were constructed of sheet-molded compound (SMC). Stamped aluminum panels formed the sleeper compartment, while fasteners adapted from aircraft technology added to the truck's strength and appearance. Inside the cab were new electronic displays, an easy-maintenance climate control system, and computer and cellular phone options undreamed of in previous trucks. A new suspension system reduced overall weight and at the same time improved ride and stability.

The T2000 was introduced at the May 1996 Kenworth dealers conference in Palm Springs, California, and it handsomely met dealers' expectations. The truck posted a 6 percent improvement in air drag coefficient.

Kenworth formally presented its new model two weeks later at the International Trucking Show in Las Vegas. One of the first orders came from H&R Transport, of Lethbridge, Alberta, which bought twenty trucks. H&R president Al Foder reported that when they were delivered to his company at the end of 1996, "everyone wanted to drive them." By the time the first

Opposite: A 1996 T2000 cab utilizing aluminum and sheet-molded compound (SMC) bonded construction.

Previous pages: 1997 Model T2000 at Fisherman's Wharf in Seattle, Washington.

149

T2000s began rolling off the assembly line, the backlog of orders exceeded 1,200. By the end of its first year, T2000 sales justified the company's $100 million investment in its development.

Shortly after the introduction of the T2000, Charles Pigott retired as PACCAR chairman. His long tenure as chief executive officer (1965 - 1996) afforded Kenworth consistent leadership, values, and vision. His son Mark, a veteran of nearly twenty years in truck manufacturing, became PACCAR's top officer.

THE COMPANY THAT BEGAN as a one-shop pioneer truck builder has grown to become a global manufacturer. By the beginning of 1998—its seventy-fifth year—Kenworth was producing trucks in the United States at two Washington state locations, Seattle and Renton, and at a large plant in Chillicothe, Ohio. Kenworth was also manufacturing trucks in three plants outside the United States: Mexicali, Mexico; Bayswater, Victoria, Australia; and Xuzhou, Jiangsu, China.

Kenworth's venerable Seattle plant has produced trucks since 1946. The plant produces subassemblies and fabricated parts for Kenworth's nearby Renton facility. It also manufactures off-highway trucks for both domestic and export markets, including the C500 and 953 series. The size and custom-built nature of very large trucks, like the C500 and some 953s, mean they are best stall-built, one at a time.

The Renton plant was built in 1993 on the site of PACCAR's original rail car plant. Its assembly line, snaking through part of the 270,000 square feet of manufacturing space, produces T600, T800, and W900 models. It was the first Kenworth plant to be equipped with an electrostatic painting system, enabling a more even application of coatings to cabs, frames, and fabricated parts.

The largest Kenworth plant, built in Chillicothe in 1973, is the only Kenworth plant to build the T2000. It also produces T600, T800, and W900 models, and from time to time stall-builds off-road models. It was originally designed to produce up to twenty trucks a day. However, by 1998, thanks to a series of innovative additions, it has produced as many as forty-six trucks on a single shift. This production rate was made possible in part by a unique application of robots to construct flawless T2000 cabs with composite materials and bonding agents.

Kenworth has produced trucks in Canada since 1927. Prior to 1955, Kenworth trucks were assembled in Canada on a contract basis with heavy equipment manufacturers. Kenworth began building trucks at Ste.-Therese in 1971, and over the years the plant became an integral part of Kenworth's production for East Coast markets. In 1992, the company's Class 7 manufacturing was moved from Brazil to Ste.-Therese, where the K300 was built until economic conditions resulted in temporary closing of the 300,000-square-foot plant. As the Canadian economy became more favorable for manufacturing, capital improvements were made at Ste.-Therese, with plans to re-open in 1999.

Kenworth is the best-selling Class 8 truck in Mexico, with most of the vehicles manufactured in a large, modern manufacturing facility at Mexicali, near the California border. The Mexicali plant produces T600 and T800 models for the Mexican and South American markets and T300 models for markets worldwide.

Outside North America, Kenworth began producing trucks in Bayswater, Victoria, Australia, in 1970. The plant builds extra-heavy-duty highway and off-road conventional and COE-model trucks for the demanding conditions of Australia, New Zealand, and New Guinea. Australian trucks are often powered by 650-horsepower diesel engines for pulling "road trains" sometimes as long as 160 feet.

The company has entered into several international assembly agreements. In 1996, through PACCAR International, Kenworth joined Chinese-owned Xuzhou Construction Machinery Group to assemble trucks for the growing Chinese construction market. Kenworth had previously been involved in international joint-venture agreements, first in Malaysia, then in Zimbabwe, and more recently in Russia.

By the time of Kenworth's celebration of its seventy-fifth anniversary, it had become the most recognized name in heavy-duty truck manufacturing worldwide.

FROM ITS EARLIEST DAYS, Kenworth understood the powerful argument for quality. In 1923, when Kenworth was formed—and even earlier, with its predecessor, Gersix—truck quality was measured by strength and durability. Comfort, economy, and serviceability came later.

Kenworth quality has always thrived on close links between the company's customers and its engineers. Beginning in the 1920s, that link was salesman Vernon Smith, who scribbled out manufacturing specifications on scraps of paper following meetings with dealers and customers. He attached his jottings to orders for new trucks—some costing as much as $2,000—and handed them to chief engineer John Holmstrom, who refined the buyer's requirements into engineering language, and then bench-built and delivered the trucks, sometimes in person.

Kenworth's legacy is studded with innovations such as the first diesel, the first sleeper, the first cab-over-engine truck, and the torsion-bar suspension system. Kenworth's advancements in aerodynamics have given its trucks a wide reputation for fuel economy. The company's pioneering work in developing the aerodynamic T600 has altered every engineer's approach to truck design, and the T2000 is expected to have a similar impact on the industry.

Innovation back in the 1920s could mean something as basic as adding windshield wipers, side panels, or doors. These early trucks have long since earned a place in museums and collectors' garages. Seventy-five years from now, a Kenworth classic such as the T2000 will no doubt be on museum display, and drivers of the late twenty-first century will chuckle at the truck's "old-fashioned" look and lack of sophistication. But like Buster Arnestad when he came across the old Gersix that he later restored, they will marvel at its quality.

Museum visitors may even sense the spirit of Vernon Smith behind the truck, waiting for his next customer. "Tell us what you want," he'd say, "and we'll build it. We'll make sure it does the job and makes you the most money. It'll be the favorite truck in your fleet."

155

Vernon Smith at his Mercer Street desk during the 1930s.

No photography permitted